The Rules of School

Educational Change and Development Series

Series Editors: Andy Hargreaves, Ontario Institute for Studies in Education, Canada and
Ivor F. Goodson, Warner Graduate School, University of Rochester, USA and Centre for Applied Research in Education, University of East Anglia, Norwich, UK

Re-schooling Society
David Hartley

The Gender Politics of Educational Change
Amanda Datnow

The Rules of School Reform
Max Angus

The Rules of School Reform

Max Angus

 The Falmer Press

(A member of the Taylor & Francis Group)
London • Washington, D.C.

UK	Falmer Press, 1 Gunpowder Square, London, EC4A 3DE
USA	Falmer Press, Taylor & Francis Inc., 1900 Frost Road, Suite 101, Bristol, PA 19007

First published in 1998

A catalogue record for this book is available from the British Library

ISBN 0 7507 0637 6 cased
ISBN 0 7507 0638 4 paper

Library of Congress Cataloging-in-Publication Data are available on request

Jacket design by Caroline Archer

Typeset in 10/12pt Garamond by
Graphicraft Typesetters Ltd., Hong Kong.

Printed in Great Britain by Biddles Ltd., Guildford and King's Lynn on paper which has a specified pH value on final paper manufacture of not less than 7.5 and is therefore 'acid free'.

Contents

For James, Robert and Beth

Preface

I doubt whether I have ever met a colleague who could not venture an opinion about what needed to be done to make schools better. I am the same. I acquired this outlook first as a teacher and later an official for more than twenty years in a state education department where I became involved in a constant flow of new policies and programs designed to improve the public education system and the schools within it. Some were small scale and local, others national. Along with my colleagues, I came to believe whole-heartedly in the ethic that school 'improvement' was in fact a good thing.[1] The fact that most of the ideas failed to come to fruition was taken merely as a sign of the importance of trying harder. In fact, I came to accept this process of trying new ideas and subsequently shedding them to be a natural phenomenon. Although this was as predictable as the seasons, it was not then evident to me that constant change amid enduring regularities was a permanent feature of the system.

I will illustrate this pattern with four brief stories drawn from my experience. I expect that any person closely involved with schools over the past thirty years could produce similar stories though I recognize that, depending on where the author was situated in the 'system', the stories might have a different perspective and, perhaps, a different moral. I have chosen these four because they represent some of the different premises that have guided reform attempts. I have called the four stories 'reform by proclamation', 'structural reform', 'grass-roots reform' and 'regulatory reform'. Each consumed the depleted reserves of energy and good will of thousands of teachers and officials. None succeeded in achieving their fundamental purposes. We were too busy moving on to the next to learn from the last yet these experiences and years of reflection have provided much of the grist from which my argument about school regulation and change has developed.

Reform by Proclamation

My first story is about a piece of paper issued in the early 1970s when the progressive education movement was in full swing. I recall being struck with admiration for a Director General of Education from another State who issued a proclamation to school principals in 1970 (see Jones, 1970).

> I have been asked to define more clearly what is meant by the freedom you and your staff have been exhorted to use in your schools.

After this great opening it continued:

> Let me say at the outset that you as Head of your school, by delegated authority from the Minister and the Director General, are in undisputed control of your school. Within the broad framework of the Education Act, the general curriculum advised by curriculum boards and approved by me, the Director General of Education, and the general policy set by your Division and communicated to you by circular, you have the widest liberty to vary courses, to alter the timetable, to decide on the organisation of the school and the government within the school, to experiment with teaching methods, assessment of student achievement and in extra curricular activities.

The appeal in the Memorandum — to abandon as soon as possible the orthodox, fixed timetable and the strictly regulated movement of staff and students as the blueprint of the school day — has been echoed by most school reformers since.

Over the years, I have read many official memoranda. This one is my all time favourite. I can recall first reading it and being filled with envy, wishing my own Director General had shown such leadership. As a young man, I interpreted the Memorandum to mean that principals had enormous scope to introduce changes to their schools without requiring the Education Department's approval and, further, that it was no longer acceptable for principals encountering problems to blame someone else or expect someone from the bureaucracy to solve them. Principals and teachers were responsible for the running of their schools. Freed by the Memorandum, they would create new forms of schooling.

Whether its claims were literally true or not, or even perceived by anyone other than myself to be so, is hard to determine. Over twenty-five years later, heads of state education departments are still issuing reports and memoranda which purport to offer schools freedom and responsibility yet continue to get a lukewarm response. Looking back, it seems naive to have imagined that sending teachers edicts about freedom would make them free.

Structural Reform

My second story, also drawn from the 1970s, is about bricks and mortar, physical structures that tangibly shape schools. Impressed by reports of English primary schools of open plan design, we built huge barn-shaped school buildings containing largely undifferentiated space accommodating the equivalent of eight classrooms. These were called open area schools and were meant to encourage the flexible grouping of students rather than uniform-sized classes. The buildings appeared wherever there was a need for a new school or the refurbishing of an old one. A great deal of energy was thrown behind the innovation. The rationale for the buildings was plain; senior officials knew what they wanted:

a different kind of teaching and learning, the kind that most progressive educators the world over wanted, and they thought, by providing the buildings and in-service training courses that teachers would realize a dream.

As a junior research officer, I was fully committed to the open area concept; at the time it seemed as though the nature of primary school education was about to change, for the better, of course. The disappointments came some years later when I participated in a national evaluation of the new school design. By the time we had finished our study in 1979, the reform had been overtaken by events: teachers were building make-shift partitions to restore the classroom configuration they were used to and school authorities were pulling back from their commitment to the concept. Our report, which suggested that there were serious problems with the way the school buildings were being used, mostly served to confirm what the majority of teachers and officials already knew: the main thing that had changed was the buildings. The different kind of teaching and learning which had been its rationale proved more elusive (see Angus *et al.*, 1979).[2]

Grass-roots Reform

During my career in the Education Department I became its representative on a state-level committee established to disburse Federal Government funds to innovative, worthwhile school projects. The Innovations Program, as the initiative was known, was intended to promote more diversity in public education systems with respect to school organization, curriculum and pedagogy. It encouraged participants to bypass the state education bureaucracies which were perceived to be unsympathetic to ideas for school improvement that were formulated by local schools and their communities. My job was to make sure that the Education Department's interests were protected. To my surprise it was not a particularly demanding job because there were relatively few projects that threatened the sovereignty of the Department.

The Innovations Program ran for seven years and enabled many fine projects to get off the ground. It had little impact on system-level policy. The only example that I can recall was in the area of school bus policy. The program provided a precedent and then the dam burst; henceforth, schools could purchase and maintain their own school buses instead of hiring them. This may have been considered a victory from the point of view of the Federal officials in the national capital but was hardly worthy of a champagne celebration in the overall scheme of things.

This was the time when the advocacy for 'grass roots' change was in the ascendant and it was widely held that successful school reform could only be accomplished if the departmental bureaucrats who stood in the way of progress were bypassed or ignored.[3] Again, looking back, the whole program seems well-intentioned but naive. The structures that constituted the public education system were unshaken by this reform attempt.

Regulatory Reform

In 1991, I became my Minister's representative on the Governing Board of the National Project for the Quality of Teaching and Learning. It was a high-powered Board, containing senior officials representing state employers, national and state union leaders, senior Federal Government and trade union officials as well as representatives from the private school sector.

I saw the Project as an opportunity to make use of the lessons about reform I had learned from past experience. These were lessons I had come to see as negative. This time, we were able to incorporate into the design of the Project many of the features recommended by experts about educational change: the principal stake holders were officially represented and in a position to steer the Project; traditional antagonists, the unions and employers, were both backing the Project; teachers could direct their own reform activities; and, of particular interest to me by that stage, there was a commitment to exempt participating schools from restrictive rules. The Project would adopt a blend of what the literature referred to as 'top–down' and 'grass roots' change strategies.

A core issue within the Project was whether innovative approaches to teaching were being restricted by the conditions of work specified in industrial awards and agreements.[4] The Governing Board for the Project decided to test the adequacy of the regulatory framework, including departmental regulations as well as those produced by the industrial relations system. The vehicle was to be the National Schools Project. The method was to invite 170 pilot schools from among all states and territories to develop plans for improving teaching and learning and, in the event that the implementation of the plan was likely to be obstructed by a rule or regulation, invite the pilot schools to apply for exemption from it. This way the Board members would learn which regulations were impeding innovative teaching practices and what were the likely consequences of abolishing the regulations. It was expected by me and by at least some other members of the Board that by the end of the Project there would be sufficient evidence to support an overhaul of the whole regulatory system. In this way other schools would benefit from the experience of the Project schools.

What happened? There were many interesting school projects and a few exemptions but there was no regulatory reform. Union and departmental officials agreed that the National Schools Project demonstrated that regulations were not restricting teachers from trying more innovative work practices. It was 'culture' that curbed professional adventurousness in teachers. I was disappointed. It was my dissatisfaction with the answer to this question that has motivated me to write this book.

Might Regulation Be the Answer?

As I look back on episode after episode of attempted school reform — proclamations of freedom, new school designs, innovations programs and regulatory waivers are several of many in which I have been involved — I feel a compulsion to ask: What went wrong? Why did they consistently fall short of the mark? My colleagues who participated with me are never short of an answer but none satisfies me. Recently, I have come to believe that regulation is at the heart of it. In fact, in each of my stories of reform the events could be reframed in terms of reformers engaging, or failing to engage with, rule systems: the proclamation ignored them; the open plan design produced some changes but left many powerful rules intact; the innovations projects changed informal rules but left other official rules intact; the waiver project enabled some official rules to change but other tacit expectations were kept firmly in place.

Initially, the official rules of the system, that is, the education acts and regulations, seemed unrelated to the buzzing school reform activity in which my colleagues and I were absorbed. However, the longer I worked in the system and the more senior the position I held, the more I became aware of the official rules and the way they functioned, so often appearing to block the reform attempts that I worked to implement. Among the more salient examples were the rules embedded in the industrial agreements between the teacher union and education department, agreements, for example, relating to class size maxima or the teacher transfer and promotion system. I began to recognize that if a reform were to have any chance of success it would need to fit within the rules held to be important by the union and department officials who negotiated these agreemens. I also became aware of just how much scope these same departmental officials had for interpreting the rules, particularly in terms of when they ought to be, or not be, invoked.

Later, as an academic, it appeared to me that the official rules were overlooked in theoretical explanations of why so many school reforms failed to endure. The study of official rules was traditionally conducted under such rubrics as 'legal studies' or 'education and the law' where the law was seen as an inert body of legal 'facts' rather than as an instrument that was used dynamically in contests over change.

My problem was that I could not fully explain how the official rules supported certain ways of doing things and pre-empted others. If people were unaware of the official rules, or even denied that they were constrained by them, how could I substantiate what intuitively I felt to be otherwise, namely that the official rules, together with informal rules, constituted the core structures that held the system in place and maintained the status quo?

Notes

1 Lundgren refers to this disposition as 'social meliorism'. Historians Tyack and Cuban convey a similar sentiment with respect to school reform in the United States. They see the history of school reform as a history of teachers and officials responding to utopian expectations of what schools can do.

2 There was no explicit reference to the issue of regulation in our final report. There was a comment, however, on the dilemma confronting departmental officials whereby

they were required to administer uniform conditions for teacher employment and at the same time promote flexibility of school organization and innovative teaching approaches.

3   The Innovations Program was one of several launched by the Federal Government through the newly created Australian Schools Commission. The Directors General at the time regarded the Australian Schools Commission as a highly intrusive agency of the Federal Government: though they wanted its funding they sought to elude its control. As public education is administered by the states the Directors General held the trump cards: they made the rules for schools. The political context for the Innovations Program is described in Dudley *et al.*, 1995.

4   For a comprehensive discussion of the industrial relations system in Australia and its impact on teachers and teaching see Seddon, 1996.

Acknowledgments

Before moving on to the argument of the book I wish to thank the many colleagues who contributed to its completion.

Some of the ideas in this book have been gestating for nearly a decade. I am no longer sure how they all began. I am sure, however, that many have been appropriated unconsciously from discussions with others or from reading their work. Though I cannot identify all of my sources I am able to acknowledge some.

I am particularly indebted to Harriet Olney. She has edited each draft of the book and enhanced it in every respect. There is a fine line between author and editor and Harriet would often cross it by reformulating what I wrote in such a way that original ideas were transformed. This book is her achievement as well as mine.

Brendon Davies and his colleagues at Willetton Senior High School deserve special mention. I have tried to tell as impartially as possible what happened in Brendon's school in Chapter 9 though I have not sought to disguise that I am highly admiring of him and what he attempted to do in his school. It is a story that in many respects ought have been told by Brendon. I appreciate his openness and permission to interpret what happened from my perspective.

I appreciate very much the other teachers and officials who volunteered their time and talked candidly with me. For the most part I have preserved their anonymity as a consequence of our initial agreement. Hence, I cannot acknowledge them by name. This is unfortunate as too often participation in research is a thankless task.

I would like to acknowledge the support of colleagues who were members of the National Project on the Quality of Teaching and Learning that functioned between 1991–3. In particular, I acknowledge Ken Boston, Sharan Burrow, Laurie Carmichael, Frank Coolahan, Rob Durbridge, Wal Jurkiewicz, Dianne Peacock, Lynne Rolley, Alan Ruby, Max Sawatzki, David Tonkin and Greg Taylor. For the duration of the Project we shared a vision that transcended our factional interests.

Andy Hargreaves pulled the trigger for the book and urged me to take the first step and submit a book proposal. If it had not been for his encouragement I might still have been muddling over interview transcripts.

The book was first drafted while I was on study leave at the College of Education at Michigan State University. Anne Schneller and David Bolig assisted me while I was ensconced in the IRT library. Philip Cusick, Bob Floden,

Trudy Sykes, Gary Sykes and Suzanne Wilson provided intellectual and social support.

My thinking was helped by my various conversations with Ray Knight and Michael Daly who explored similar interests in masters dissertations which I supervised.

Several friends provided helpful comments on drafts of this book and made useful suggestions. I am indebted to Lois Achimovich, Dean Ashenden, Jane Figgis, Jan Gray, Peter Hamilton, Andy Hargreaves, Sandra Milligan, Gary Sykes and Suzanne Wilson for their help via this means.

In 1989, I participated in a local waiver project which in some respects was a precursor to the National Schools Project. Though the project was eventually abandoned after two years it provided an action research basis for exploring the power of regulation. Roy Gilbert, Peter Hamilton and Harriet Olney participated in this.

Joe Rees was a director in the Ontario Ministry of Education in Toronto where I spent a year on exchange during 1978 in the Supervision and Legislation Branch. On a subsequent exchange in 1991, Joe worked with me on a review of the regulations in the Western Australian Education Department. In 1996, Joe arranged for me to visit again the Ontario Ministry of Education where I met with Anne Church and John Tomlinson who briefed me on the Ontario Education Act. I am grateful for Joe's assistance throughout our long association.

I would also like to thank Michael Warren of the Legal Services Bureau in the Michigan State Department who patiently explained to me the workings of the Michigan regulatory framework.

Finally, I would like to acknowledge Ruben Carriedo whom I met in 1991 at the San Diego City Schools District Office. The visit was formative in my thinking.

The research was made possible by two Edith Cowan University research grants awarded in 1993 and 1996.

1   Introduction

> Being free and unfree at the same time is perhaps the most common of our experiences. It is also arguably the most confusing. (Bauman, 1990)

The Argument

In the stacks of books written about educational change authors commonly wonder why attempts to change the way that schools function are so short-lived. Somehow or other, after a period of experimentation the system returns to stasis. The more things change the more they stay the same.[1] Various plausible reasons are posited and examined to explain the stasis but they seldom include the rules and regulations among the contributory factors.

In this book, I use the interplay of regulation, culture and power to explain why fundamental change has been elusive. The argument is complex and there are several twists and turns. This is because there are several paradoxes to explain. For example, although school reform is often predicated upon regulatory change, the body of official rules in school systems maintains the status quo. Further, I contend that teaching is governed by official rules even though there are relatively few that pertain explicitly to instruction and pedagogy. Another paradox is that even when given the opportunity, teachers rarely seek exemptions from the official rules. Finally, I maintain that although teachers have only a sketchy knowledge of the official rules it is also true that these same rules are a powerful instrument of control. I address each of these paradoxes.

In this chapter, I have three purposes. The first is to clarify what I mean by reform. On a number of counts the term 'reform' is problematic yet it is in the title of the book and I rely on it throughout. My second purpose is to explain the approach I adopted when investigating the nexus between regulation and reform. Finally, I will provide a brief synopsis of my argument.

What Is School Reform?

The term 'school reform' is almost a cliché. It commonly implies 'improvement' so that the terms 'school reform' and 'school improvement' are usually taken to be synonymous. This need not be the case. The benefits of a reform may be in the eye of the beholder, perceived rather than real. Many teachers have quite jaundiced views of school reform. Hence, although I continue to refer generally to reform, and have already confessed to being a confirmed reformer in my past, in my use of the term in this book, I am agnostic. This is not because I think the motives behind reform are irrelevant or that change is self-evidently good and therefore not a matter deserving of elaboration, but because the issue is outside the scope of this book. To take an example, the 1988 Education Reform Act was hugely unpopular among educators in Britain. I accept that there were many good reasons for this condemnation but have not been persuaded against using the Reform Act as an example of the indirect relationship between legislation and pedagogy because of this. It is a good example of this relationship. I have not sought to examine its merit as a reform.

The word 'reform' also commonly implies change on a grand scale that occurs over months, perhaps years. The term 'school reformer', unless defined inclusively, has a pompous, arrogant ring. The act of a teacher taking initiative as an individual, would not usually be paid sufficient attention to count as reform. In my definition, however, I include local and individual acts as school reform. Hence, I include among school reformers teachers, parents, even students, not just the politicians and bureaucrats who direct structural realignments.

Further, by my definition, school reform is a deliberate, planned intervention to improve some aspect of the operation of schools. I differentiate it from unsought-for change that impacts on a school. For example, a school timetable may need to be changed to fit into new public transport timetables. The change was not introduced to improve the school's operation though it is possible that it inadvertently does so. School reform is also different from cultural change that affects society generally and that produces almost imperceptible modifications to schools: dress codes, architectural styles, racial attitudes, uses of leisure time, and so on. Schools are continually changing without any prompting from school reformers.

Most school reform that has been the subject of some kind of evaluation has been of the large scale, top–down variety. One reason for this is that this has been the dominant means by which government officials thought they could bring about change. Another is that this mode catches the public and professional interest. It is easier to study such work than the persistent efforts of individual teachers however impressive these might be. Reforms of the top–down variety also feature in this study, not because they are assumed to be inherently good and therefore deserving of study but because they frequently involve some adjustment of the official rules. However, I am also interested in school initiated reforms that have been designed to fit within the existing structure of rules.

A final point about school reform is that there have been very few attempts to abolish altogether the structures that hold traditional patterns of teaching and learning in place. Reformers have generally sought to change single structures — my story about open plan school design is a case in point

— but there have been few systematic attempts to redesign from scratch schools within public education systems. It has been easier to establish schools outside the structures, as is presently occurring with charter schools, than re-configure the systemic structures. Such so-called lighthouse schools, I predict, will eventually be reclaimed by the system and the structures that they sought to evade will spring back into place unless reform can be construed differently.

My Approach

It surprises me that the way in which the rules 'work' has been largely overlooked by researchers trying to understand the nature of school reform. I am not sure why. It may be that the study of rules is no longer fashionable; interest in this area seems to have diminished during the 1960s and 1970s. It is also possible, that researchers still study rules though they call them something else: the topic of power, for example, has attracted interest. It may also be the case that the research community has concluded that the notion of schools as rule-governed institutions is a myth and as a consequence rules cannot explain why school reform does or does not work. Such a conclusion, however, runs counter to everyday experience in which our actions are shaped by rules. I am more inclined to believe that because rules are all-pervasive they have become a taken-for-granted part of the school reform landscape. This has happened, in my view, because school reform has been bracketed as something separate from everyday experience when, in fact, for most of the time it is part of the humdrum of working life.

How to proceed with my investigation? One approach would be to take a rule and consider it in isolation from the body of rules from which it is drawn. For example, a particular piece of legislation, or a specific regulation or ordinance might be examined to see whether it has been observed, how it was interpreted, the scope of discretion exercised in its execution, the consequences of non-compliance and so on. There have been some helpful studies of this kind to which I will later refer. Most, however, tend to ignore or understate the significance of vast networks of rules that form the regulatory and cultural context (see Wilson, 1988).[2] Examining 'Big R' regulation, without reference to the other rules that come into play reveals only part of the picture. Therefore, my inclination is to examine systems of rules. The methods that I have employed in the study and the data sources are discussed in the appendix on methodology.

Swedish sociologists Tom Burns and Helena Flam have come closest to reaching a synthesis, which they called 'system rule theory,' to which I will refer in some detail later, but even this work is now only a partial synthesis as it does not take account of post-structuralist perspectives which have emerged recently in sociology (Burns and Flam, 1987). But it is more complicated even than that. The study of rules is not the sole preserve of sociologists. Rules have also been a topic of long-standing interest to philosophers and legal theorists.

In fact, in practically all branches of the social sciences and humanities scholars have at some time or other become engaged by the relationship between rules and human conduct.

As I sought to understand the outcome of the National Schools Project, in addition to rule systems, I began to draw on the constructs of culture and power to explain the stability and uniformity of school practice. These constructs were not incompatible with system rule theory though they had separate disciplinary roots and provided entry points to structuralist and post-structuralist thinking. The exercise of power seemed to be at the crux of what I was seeking to find out but power need not be exercised solely through a 'legal-rational' rule system.

I became engaged by the idea of special rules about how rules are applied which I call meta-rules. These implicit rules about how to use collectivities of rules serve an executive function, according to my formulation. They, rather than the official rules that appear in handbooks, signal what needs to be done in general terms and how to approach the official rules. The meta-rules are embedded in the departmental 'discourse' that is used by teachers and officials to explain what they are doing and why they must do it. It is these meta-rules, containing a shared understanding and expectations of how the system is to operate, which provide the stability more so than any official edict. School reform, I contend, is governed ultimately by meta-rules.

An Overview of the Argument

The Problem

There are two main questions from which all the other questions raised are drawn. These are:

1 Why have so many aspects of school and classroom life been so robust in the face of attempts to change them? and
2 What role do official rules play in maintaining school systems which support teaching and learning in their current dominant forms?

The Official Rules

There is an extraordinary number of official rules that circumscribe what should happen in schools, so many that it is improbable that any single person could know all the rules that apply in even one system. The prospect of ever knowing the corpus of rules is made more difficult because of its organic nature: rules are constantly being added while others are falling into disuse. The condition of the corpus is partly explained by the multiple sources of authorship from both within and without the school system. The rules keep being generated because there is a strong belief among officials and teachers that problems can be solved by creating new rules. I contend that the state of the corpus of rules has important implications for school reform.

Regulation and Teaching

Juxtaposed against the extensiveness of official rules is an absence of official rules about teaching. However, despite this absence of rules relating directly to instruction and pedagogy, teachers are in fact constrained by the combined effect of numerous rules which are one or more steps removed. On the surface, the experience of constraints that are not immediately evident appears to be a paradox but with closer scrutiny impinging factors can be identified. I argue that regulation rarely intrudes directly into the instructional aspects of teachers' work but functions like a shell around it providing an external limit of what is possible.

School Reform As Re-regulation

Most school reform involves some degree of re-configuring of the official rules even though this may not be overt. Generally, accounts of reform mention any initial regulatory changes and then, from that point onwards, ignore the interplay of rules. The new rules are presumed to mesh together smoothly with existing rules. This presumption is made without reformers or those investigating reforms taking account of the imbalance between the corpus of rules as a whole and the small proportion of rules which have been adjusted.

In studies where researchers have continued to scrutinize the regulatory system during the period in which a reform is implemented it has been observed that the official rules have been transformed during this process.

Rule Systems

In developing a theoretical basis for my argument, I found it necessary to differentiate between collections of rules in which official rules interact with informal rules and those which are limited to those with official status. In the case of the latter group, I use the term 'rule regime' to refer to collectivities of official rules related to particular tasks or fields of activities. Even with this restriction, such regimes can be extensive and difficult to map. I use the term 'informal rules' to refer to local rules that have no official status in an organizational sense but which signal how people are expected to relate to each other, undertake tasks and so on. These informal rules combine with official rules to form social rule systems. School reform is shaped more by these social rule systems than by any individual rule or literal interpretation of a set of official rules.

I argue that to ascribe to a single rule the power to produce an intended response in a complex social situation without reference to the web of related, existing rules, is an act of folly. This statement applies equally to formal and informal rules.

Culture and Regulation

In the symbolic world of teachers, official rules are an artefact of immense cultural significance. I explain how the official rules constitute part of school culture; they are not separate from it. Within this context, the distinctions between official rules and informal rules become blurred. It does not follow that because many teachers are not familiar with the detail of most official rules that they have no effect. Although an unknown individual rule may have no effect, this does not undermine the cultural significance of the corpus of rules.

I argue that it is misleading to present law and culture as two distinct entities because the law is an important aspect of culture. Therefore, the proposition that cultural changes can occur without reference to official rules is spurious.

Power and Rules

The purpose of most rules is to direct the actions of employees and limit the power of officials. In practice, it seldom works this way. The official rules are an instrument of power. Personal judgments determine when they can be ignored or invoked. This is particularly the case when the legal framework is not generally well understood and there is a dependency upon those with authority.

Education systems run smoothly when the power relationships between employers and employees are stable. School reform, however, is likely to disturb the balance of power. When this occurs, official rules can be brought into play, particularly so when one side wishes to block the other. Power struggles can be fought out within the micro-politics of school staff rooms, through legal challenges to courts or by the manoeuvrings of political parties in legislatures.

Meta-rules

People need guidance to help them make decisions about when it is appropriate to ignore or invoke a rule. This guidance is provided by 'rules about rules' which I call meta-rules. Meta-rules are often tacit and derive much of their power from this quality. They relate to the official rule system but are not a part of it. Generally, school reformers do not take account of them. However, because meta-rules tend to support notions about fairness and, as a consequence, the rectitude of established practices they can be more persuasive than edicts.

In Chapter 9, I illustrate how meta-rules work in practice with a case study of a suburban high school which initiated its own reforms and in doing so contravened systemic meta-rules. I contend that the school experienced what many schools confront when they push the limits of systemic control.

The Rules of School Reform

There are three parts to my answer to the questions I posed when defining the problem I have addressed. First, a 'protective' shell of rules has developed around teaching. This shell allows modest variation to pedagogy but only within the limits it defines.

Second, attempts to modify established practices are enveloped by existing social rule systems. This is made possible by a failure to recognize the significance of the totality of rules and inadequate scrutiny of the manner in which rules interact with one another.

Third, the carapace around teaching is held in place by meta-rules which culturally inscribe and situate the participants in school systems in power relationships. These relationships tend to be self-regulating and so self-perpetuating.

Under these conditions, the regularities of schooling seem set to endure indefinitely. It would take a major shift in the power relations between unions and employers, employers and employees, and between schools and their lay communities before the scaffolding of rules that supports the shell could be dismantled and reconstructed.

Notes

1 This is a common refrain in the literature on school reform. See for example, Cohen, 1988.
2 Within the body of research on rules the question of how the rules are called into play continues to be a contentious issue. Some theorists, for example, have adopted a highly rational construction of the world: an actor enters a social situation, recognizes which rules are applicable and acts accordingly. In this instrumentalist construction precisely stated rules, backed with legitimate authority, control behaviour. I find this perspective to be simplistic. My position is not that rules are bad — they may or may not be — nor that clarity is to be eschewed, but that the world does not function in such a straight forward manner as rule makers seem to believe. A direct relationship between a rule and a person's response to it is too limited a theory to be of use in most situations; such relationships cannot helpfully be compared to the smell of food causing Pavlov's dog to salivate although they have been represented as such. This thinking, much influenced by Weber's classic theory of bureaucracy, underpins the popular maxim that clearly-stated rules lead to better governance.

2   Official Rules

Our present social structure was generated by the often conflicting actions of countless individual attempts to adjust to the circumstances of human existence. There is no mind that can comprehend it in its entirety and impose a conceptual unity upon it. Our law mirrors our society. (Christie, 1982)

Introduction

The regulatory systems which I am seeking to understand, while incorporating 'the law', include rules which have not been derived from legal statutes or been codified according to the steely logic of the law. Nevertheless, because conventionally we think about the application of the official rules in legal terms, the full range of rules needs to be considered within a legal framework.

My purpose in this chapter is to describe the body of official rules and regulations that are used to govern a school system. There are too many to simply catalogue: the official rules are found in all kinds of places and number thousands. Hence, I will describe how a corpus of rules is structured and provide examples of different kinds of rules. It is my intention to map the broad outline of the totality of rules which surround public schools in sufficient detail to enable readers to make sense of the accounts of how rules are used.

The legal frameworks for school governance differ among countries. Some of the differences are structural, for example, some countries have nationally administered public education systems whereas others have state or regional patterns of administration. Other differences in the legal frameworks are procedural where, for example, arrangements for particular administrative functions such as staff selection or school financing differ. As well, there are differences in the technical and colloquial languages used to describe the regulatory system. Finally, there are cultural differences, some of which are quite subtle; for example, teachers and officials may have different attitudes towards authority, compliance and the role of central government. It is my contention that although all systems vary to some extent, the official rules that govern school systems in western democracies are more similar than different. Though the description of official rules that follows may not apply universally it is sufficiently exact to serve my purposes of showing how rules shape the response of schools to educational change (see Birch, 1976; Chisolm, 1987; Knott, Tronc and Middleton, 1980).[1]

Most of the examples that I use to illustrate the official rules are Australian. The conclusions that I reach regarding the condition of the regulating systems and the uses made of the official rules are based on my examination of Australian systems and may not apply universally though they appear generally valid for Michigan in the United States and Ontario in Canada, two other regulatory systems with which I am familiar. The official rules, though differing in detail, serve similar regulatory functions in these jurisdictions.

The Official Rules about Education with a Statutory Basis

For the purposes of this descriptive analysis of official rules intended to support the administration of public education systems it is helpful to divide the official rules into four hierarchical levels according to the status and generality of the rules. These are:

1   education statutes;
2   subsidiary legislation;
3   administrative instructions issued by education departments and school districts; and
4   school rules.

These layers, or categories of rules, are common to most public education systems, although terminology varies somewhat.

Education Statutes

Education statutes passed by state or national parliaments form the core legislation which defines the administrative structures which are used to govern public education. An education statute can be expected to describe the powers of the politician who has responsibility for an education portfolio in a cabinet and, where there is a separate office, the head of the education agency which has the responsibility for administering the public education system.[2] Because education statutes allocate powers, they are the most likely starting point for a legal analysis of any official rules. Although other acts of parliament may be pertinent, for example, industrial relations acts, public sector management acts and equal opportunity acts, these are not as central to the administration of school systems as are the education statutes.[3]

For the lay person, most education statutes are not easy to read and understand. They may define a mixed bag of powers, obligations and activities. These include such things as requirements for students to attend school, the basis on which financial assistance is to be given to non-government schools, powers to appoint staff, disciplinary procedures, conditions under which students may be charged fees and the conditions under which welfare

officers may accost children in public places. In countries which have intermediate levels of administration, such as school districts accountable to school
boards, the statutes explicitly define the powers and responsibilities of these
bodies. Comparisons of education statutes drafted at different stages of this century indicate that although recent legislation is more coherent, because it lacks
the multitude of amendments which characterize older legislation, an item-by-item
comparison suggests that the content is comparable (see Shorten, 1995).

Subsidiary Legislation

Sitting beneath each education statute is the subsidiary legislation which gives
effect to it. Whereas the statutes are usually general statements, the subsidiary
legislation tends to be more specific. In Australia, the subsidiary legislation is
also known as the Parliamentary Regulations, or simply the Regulations.

Parliaments vary with respect to where they situate the rules; some have
more detailed legislation and fewer administrative directives and others vice
versa. Because of the vagaries of political processes, it is generally easier to
effect changes to subsidiary legislation than it is to legislation. Hence, officials
tend to argue that it is preferable to frame legislation in general terms and
confine the specifics to subsidiary regulation. They claim this promotes flexibility.
Politicians and interest groups, on the other hand, like to see detail in legislation. They say this makes it clear what requirements and protections are
actually in place.

Because subsidiary legislation is more likely to be concerned with detail
and is seen to be easier to change, it is at this second level that rule changes
intended to accommodate reforms are often made.

Administrative Instructions

The third layer consists of 'instructions' issued in the name of an official. These
take many forms and include memoranda, administrative circulars, policies,
guidelines, even correspondence. They may be issued from the top or administrative levels of administration. The status of these 'directives' is sometimes
ambiguous, particularly when they are presented in a format which suggests
that the intention of an author is to provide information rather than direct the
actions of employees.

In some school systems, files containing administrative directives, num-
bering hundreds of pages, are routinely issued to schools and updated when
necessary (Office of Schools Administration, Victoria, 1990; New South Wales
Department of School Education, 1993; Education Department of South Australia,
1988). These provide advice or direction on a huge range of management
matters, some dealing with bread-and-butter issues, such as leave provisions,
school bus travel or copyright restrictions whereas others appear to be either
extraordinarily trivial or arcane, for example, rules about the reporting of dead

or dying trees, or the kind of paper to be used in official correspondence. Such compendia will often be described as 'guidelines' because they purport to support and assist even though they may, in fact, be quite prescriptive.

If policy is to be placed in any level of the regulatory framework, then it ought to be placed in this third level. The difficulty in placing policy squarely in a regulatory box is that it is often couched in terms of organizational or political intentions rather than directives. For example, an education department may have a policy on student literacy which specifies levels of attainment. The policy can urge teachers but cannot reasonably direct teachers to attain those targets since their achievement may be beyond the teachers' control. Thus policy tends to enunciate expectations rather than provide directions which are acted upon. Policies often take the form of very general statements about principles to be applied in future. Sometimes their declaration mobilizes opposition enabling officials to assess the strength of feeling for and against changes before they are commenced. Because of this, most people have a wait-and-see attitude to these forms of policies.[4]

Planning statements often have an even more dubious status than policies. They may contain definitive statements about the purpose of a school system, which implies a related purpose for a school operating within it, and be issued with the endorsement of the senior officials. The extent to which staff members in schools integrate this more recent form of 'directive' depends on the extent to which they perceive such plans to be about education; documents that use the language of accountancy will generally be ignored by most school teachers and administrators even though they may be considered highly relevant to external auditors and some others. The authority of planning documents is likely to be derived from links among articulated plans, the allocation of funds and the methods used for accounting for effectiveness.

Because of the insubstantiality of much of the content of directives, policy and planning statements, they effectively lapse when they are forgotten. In some systems, this level of 'regulation' may not even be fully codified.

School Rules

There is a fourth layer: rules and directives are issued in schools by 'officials' with or without delegated authority. These take various forms — policies, procedures, codes of conduct and so on. They are incorporated into standard operating procedures for such functions as staff or student induction or absenteeism. They are meant to fit within the larger regulatory framework although it is unlikely that anyone would bother to test whether they did fit unless there were a formal complaint. Being several steps removed from the most senior official, the legal status of these 'rules' may be diminished or blurred, however, their significance for those in the school concerned may be far greater than an act of parliament.

Included in this layer are rules teachers set for students. It is not uncommon to see lists of such rules pinned on noticeboards around schools.

These rules generally state expectations about acceptable student behaviour or approaches to learning and take many forms.

The plethora of rules generated within the first, second and third levels of regulation, are commonly interpreted and restated at a local level. When this is done by officials, who have formal authority over teachers, the interpretations and restatements acquire the status of rules. Although, in a legal sense these rules may not be as significant as the legislation, subsidiary legislation and departmental directives, from the point of view of a teacher or school administrator, the school rules may be more significant if they provide crucial information about school-level practices which teachers can reasonably assume have been approved by the system.

Laws which Apply More Generally

Although the body of rules specifically designed to support the public education system is substantial, it does not contain the totality of law which has an impact on schools. Other laws which apply more generally must also be taken into consideration. These include constitutional law, judicial law and cross-sector regulatory frameworks with a statutory basis. The last of these is so extensive, containing several levels within a number of different areas, that it has been described in a section of its own. The confluence of the rules cascading from the education statutes and those that apply more generally produces a highly complex regulatory environment.

Constitutions

There is no reference to education in the national constitutions of the US, Canada and Australia. Despite this, national constitutions determine matters of great significance for schools. They make is possible for state governments to take responsibility for education and provide guidance about general matters such as individual rights and the appropriation of funds. In such federal structures, state constitutions may be more likely to refer directly to education. When individuals or interest groups challenge laws they do this by citing a state or national constitution as a higher authority and arguing that this has been breached. It is much more difficult to change a constitution than it is to change any other form of official rules.

Judicial Law

In contrast to statute law which is based on legislation which has passed through parliament, law is also made by judges on the basis of the particular circumstances of individual court cases. In legal systems with a British heritage, this is called common law. Because of its very nature, such law is not codified or easily accessible and most people, even senior public servants working within their area of expertise, need to rely on lawyers to advise them about the implications of judicial rulings.

Despite the difficulties in defining common law, teachers are confronted by it in the form of the omnipresence of their duty of care. Where a teacher–student relationship exits, a significant legal burden is placed on teachers who are required to exercise a duty of care for their students. As is the case with much of the law, duty of care means different things to different people. To some teachers and school administrators, it provides a justification for organizing schools around the supervision of students. It may also preclude activities that require students to learn from accepting increased responsibility if by doing so an increased risk is implied.

Consider the example of a 'lesson' in which students must use public transport to meet a teacher at a pre-arranged location. Even if parental permission had been obtained, this may not be an acceptable strategy because of the increased risk compared to that associated with a teacher arranging transport for the students. There may not be any law against the proposal, however, clarification about whether the risk was warranted could only occur if there were an accident, a court case and a judgment.

The common law duty of care is also cited by teachers' unions as a reason why their members alone can be held responsible for supervising students. Again, it is difficult to say whether this is justified in law except in regard to particular situations which have been tested in court.

In the US, legal action is often taken against school boards through civil courts on the basis that individual rights have not been upheld or that some form of negligence has been evident. This tendency towards litigation is not as evident in other countries although fear of litigation may apply more generally.

Cross-sector Regulatory Frameworks with a Statutory Basis

Much of the legislation governing schools has been developed without particular reference to schools. The rules generated by this legislation are devised and enforced by agencies elsewhere in the public sector and may apply to all government employees or even to all citizens. This creates a huge underside to the school regulatory system.

The Public Sector Management Framework

One of the most influential bodies of extra-education legislation is that relating to public sector management. It serves to administratively control government agencies, including big-budget education departments, and tie them more closely to treasury and cabinet priorities often with the intention of improving efficiency and effectiveness. Such legislation has lead school systems to introduce corporate planning, program management, performance management and various other devices touted in the private sector as methods for improving productivity.[5] The effects of such legislation is to place pressure on education departments to function like any other public sector agency.

The Industrial Relations Framework

In Australia, a highly centralized industrial relations system, the 'employer' of public school teachers is the Minister of Education in the state concerned and high proportions of the teaching workforce are union members. Industrial court determinations culminate in documents known as 'industrial awards' and agreements. These define the salary and working conditions of employees.

Alternatively, teachers are employed by school councils or school boards. Teachers' terms and conditions will be documented in employment contracts which can be determined through either individual or collective bargaining processes.[6]

Regardless of the system in operation, agreements between employers and employees have the status of legally binding documents which can be enforced by courts. Many of the rules governing teaching originate under the industrial relations framework rather than the education statutes. Enforcing these rules may be straight forward in cases where the matters of concern are cut and dried and almost impossible in relation to the more complex aspects of teachers' work responsibilities.

Other Relevant Legislation

A major contributor to the exponential growth of rules applying to schools has been the legislative reforms in areas such as occupational health and safety, equal opportunity, racial discrimination, freedom of information and copyright. To illustrate how these areas impact on schools, I will use the example of an act to administer occupational, health and safety requirements from Western Australian law (see Department of Occupational Health, Safety and Welfare, 1988).

The requirement that employers ensure the safety of their employees was not new, however, this requirement had not previously been the subject of an act of parliament. The introduction of the Act meant that in addition to ensuring safety, schools came to be defined as work places and so were required to elect safety representatives, establish committees with union representation and ensure that representatives attended courses on the provisions of the Act. Absurd situations developed where the safety of staff members was considered without reference to the safety of others on the work site, for example students, because only the staff were covered by the Act. This arose because the legislation was designed to apply to typical work sites. The implications for schools, that is, work sites where most of the people present are not employees, had not been considered during the drafting of the legislation.

The Content of the Official Rules

Despite the plethora of rules, there is a paucity of explicit references to matters directly pertaining to teachers' work. This may suggest a paradox: so many official rules but little to constrain teachers. Does this mean that teachers can operate independently without reference to the rules in regard to their professional responsibilities? This is a crucial question and in order to answer it the content of the official rules in relation to five key areas affecting teachers' work is outlined. These areas contain rules about:

1   instruction;
2   curriculum;
3   work organization;
4   the power of officials; and
5   disciplinary action.

Rules Regarding Instruction

The core business of schooling is teaching and learning yet few official rules specify how teaching and learning must take place. The Western Australian Regulations, for example, make only an oblique reference to teaching under the section, *Duties of teacher.*

> A teacher shall be present in primary or secondary school at least 15 minutes before the school commences in order to prepare the materials for his work and to secure good behaviour among his pupils.

> (2) A teacher shall not fail to carry out his normal teaching duties in respect of his pupils. (Regulation 31, Education Act Regulations, Education Department of Western Australia, 1960)

A more recently revised set of the Ontario Education Act Regulations, under the same heading, *Duties of teacher,* is similar.

> 20. In addition to the duties assigned to the teacher under the Act and by the board, a teacher shall,

(a) be responsible for effective instruction, training and evaluation of the progress of pupils in the subjects assigned to the teacher and for the management of the class or classes, and report to the principal on the progress of pupils on request; . . . (Regulation 298, Section 20, Ontario Education Act)

This latter example continues through to subsection (h) and contains more conditional clauses. However, it is no more specific about requiring any particular approach to teaching. Interestingly, the requirement that teachers be available 'at least fifteen minutes' before their classes is evident in both sets of Regulations.

Regulations do not usually attempt to define 'normal teaching duties'. If regulations, such as the examples given, were the only constraint on pedagogy then they would impose few restrictions. However, these are not the only source of constraint.

Rules about Curriculum

Although, methods of teaching *per se* are not usually prescribed in any formal or legal sense, teachers may experience apparently subtle pressures from other sources which lead them to teach in particular ways.

Pressures may be found in assessment procedures, prescribed textbooks, student aspirations combined with university selection procedures and curriculum frameworks. Some of these may exert pressure on teaching methods indirectly, for example, assessment procedures may pre-emptively require students to undertake practical work, present tutorial papers to their class and so on. In a similar way, teachers can be led to focus their instruction on curriculum content if assessment is primarily concerned with students' knowledge of this. This is most likely to be the case in the final years of schooling (see Mazibuko, 1996). Teachers often report that the impact of assessment at the end of the final year of schooling filters backwards and may informally shape the pedagogy of teachers in other grades.

Curriculum documents, in prescribing content, can shape pedagogy. Though they may not explicitly stipulate an approved pedagogy, the documents may *imply* appropriate methods and, through their sequencing of material, their explanations of the theory that underpins the syllabus and their illustrations of 'best practice', seek to persuade teachers to adopt a particular pedagogy.[7] Even broadly framed curriculum statements, such as national or state curriculum frameworks, should be considered part of the regulatory system. Where the adoption of the statements and adherence to their structures and content is tied to rewards, such as promotion and tenure, and sanctions, such as censure from the principal, students or parents, then such documents have the potential to shape school organization and pedagogy. These controls are not made explicit in the way that most official rules are.

Rules about Work Organization

Work organization parameters, such as class size, hours of instruction, definition of duties of teaching and non-teaching staff, shape teaching in so far as they extend or reduce the viability of particular forms of teaching. Ironically, decisions about these factors are not made with a view to promoting particular pedagogical approaches. Rather, they are driven principally by concerns about wage justice and equality of opportunity for employees. Determinations are rationalized largely on the basis that conditions which optimize staff satisfaction are likely to promote good teaching and thereby facilitate learning. Teacher satisfaction is generally defined by unions who act on behalf of teachers and is attributed great symbolic status particularly when union leaders represent their members interests in the media.

Many of the rules about work organization seem initially unrelated to pedagogy. The industrial concerns are in the fore. Consider, as an example, the matter of promotion in a school system. In a large system, the movement of staff on promotion from school to school may be controlled by an intricate collection of rules devised with attention to equity principles, levels of remuneration, career structures and working conditions. Promotions may also have a significant bearing on the programs that can be offered in a school: the loss of a key staff member might sink an innovative project whereas, on the other hand, the arrival of a promoted teacher might rescue another. This is well known yet because the effect of staff promotion and transfer on students' learning is not always easy to demonstrate, the educational considerations give way to the industrial.

Rules about the Powers of Officials

Education Acts contain the definitions of powers and the consequential accountability arrangements which form the nub of the regulatory system. Generally, in terms of the Act, a Minister of Education will have wide powers. In practice, however, public school systems are too extensive for an individual to manage or control and so responsibility is delegated down the line. Although the nature of delegations may differ, a Minister for Education is likely to retain ultimate responsibility for all employees in a school system as least in a nominal sense.[8] The effect of this is that a school principal will be responsible for most school-level decisions but, as soon as there is a matter of contention in the community or the media, the principal will be required to hand control back to the bureaucrats who will be better placed to consider the Minister's political imperatives.[9]

This tendency for matters of contention to be controlled outside schools is reinforced by regulations which require teachers to obey the lawful instructions of their line managers. Such powers could be interpreted to mean: 'Do as you are told'. In complex situations where there are several official, sometimes

contradictory, rules in effect, and in cultures where traditional forms of authority have status, such a regulation makes others superfluous.

Rules about Disciplinary Action

For many teachers, the most sensitive sections of the body of official rules are
those which enable senior officials to take disciplinary action against subordinates. It is not surprising that this is an area vigilantly patrolled by teacher unions.

Although on paper the disciplinary powers appear formidable, industrial
officers report that they are difficult to apply because of the protection unions
can offer and requirements that the processes of natural justice be applied. For
many teachers and educational administrators the processes are unfamiliar.
Few teachers are dismissed or demoted and, of those who are, some will have
committed a civil offence. Despite the fact that disciplinary rules are invoked
infrequently, they have symbolic significance. To many teachers they say, 'Watch
out or else!' On this basis they form an important part of the apparatus of control.

Rule Formation

Passing legislation is cited by governments as a sign of progress. It is a relatively inexpensive next step to establish a small group to devise related subsidiary legislation and then another group to explain its particular implications
for schools. Relative to this, there is usually little political gain to be made from
abolishing a provision or program particularly if these have acquired vocal supporters. The simplest way for bureaucrats to demonstrate that they are in control
of a domain is to generate and promulgate rules, or the softer versions of these,
policies and guidelines. Policy officers measure their professional standing by
the amount of policy they produce, believing that they are acting in the interests
of their organizations, namely guiding and clarifying appropriate conduct.[10]

A new rule can be a solution to a political problem. It would seem that
there can be a rule for every contingency. Rules can define who can teach in
a school. They can prescribe what is to be done in certain circumstances. They
can determine the basis on which schools are categorized. Different rules are
needed to cover the cleaning of schools. A rule can be generated when someone makes a mistake; it's a way a saying that we won't let that happen again.
I could go on. The number of rules that can be generated under these circumstances is virtually endless. For those actually making the rules, the question
of whether their creations have the effect they intended may be outside their
interests.

There are stronger incentives to create rules than to abolish obsolete
rules, thereby causing a basic problem of plumbing and drainage; the corpus
of rules fills up faster than it empties. Many teachers would find this claim surprising, given the apparent omnipotence of the state department in regard to

rule making. However, key sources of regulation are situated outside education departments and the originators of much of the regulation have little regard for the standard operating procedures of schools or the culture of teachers.

The Disarray of the Official Rules

Although substantial powers and protections may be found in the formal regulatory frameworks which govern school systems, the framework itself may be an ill-defined repository of rules. There is seldom any systematic scanning, from top to bottom, of the existing body of official rules. Just as the organizational structures of public education systems are segmented into bureaucratic layers so also are the rules. It is unlikely that anyone in a school system would know *all* the rules. Legal officers in the central office of state education departments may keep under close scrutiny the legislation for which they are responsible but they are much less sure of how the legislation has been translated and acted upon at district and school levels. In my experience, senior officials in education departments recognize that the state of their rule systems is unsatisfactory but are unable to address the problem.[11] This problem is not peculiar to education though the public education system does seem vulnerable to it. John Meyer refers to the problem as 'legalization', that is 'the disorderly introduction of legal authority into the educational order: instances which violate the routinized order and chain of command, which introduce new rules without their integration into the established set' (see Meyer, 1986). The 'disorder' may be produced by the decisions of courts, particularly in the US, or administrative agencies or statutory authorities any of which are capable of compelling a specific line of action outside the routinized command structure of the organization.

According to Meyer, the centralization of perceived disorders, combined with a decentralized educational order, such as that occurring in school systems devolving administrative responsibilities, increases legalization. This results in administrative expansion in state and district offices to manage the disorder and administrative complexity. In my view, it also changes the way members regard official rules. It makes the whole body of rules seem more remote which has the potential to make them more powerful because the totality is harder to understand; the system of regulation may even seem mysterious. Under these conditions the members of an organization become reliant on those with authority, acquired with insider knowledge, to tell them what to do.

Conclusion

In this chapter, I have sought to explain why the formal regulatory frameworks for public school systems tend to be so amorphous and untidy. The incoherence can partly be explained by multiple authorship of the elements in the rules system. A substantial proportion of the regulations has been generated by agencies unfamiliar with schools. Of those regulations devised within the school system, many address problems that arose in earlier epochs. Some of the rules are so out-of-date that they are plainly silly, thereby introducing an element of ambiguity regarding the status of the rest of the corpus. Some of the formal rules are prescriptive whereas others have the status of guidelines, illustrating an acceptable practice. It is often unclear which is mandatory and which is suggestive, thereby adding to the ambiguity. Under these conditions, it is not surprising to discover that most of the employees whose work practices are meant to be governed by the regulatory system do not know its contents and that senior managers do not refer to it in their work. And yet, as I will show in later chapters, the regulatory system shapes the work of schools.

Notwithstanding the seemingly chaotic state of the official rules, it is difficult to identify any unregulated facet of school system administration. At first glance, the education statutes appear to have neglected core functions of school systems — teaching and learning. However, officials with delegated powers have filled in the gaps, sometimes with explicit reference to teaching, sometimes with oblique reference, and sometimes by establishing rules one or more steps removed from the act of teaching but which nevertheless bear indirectly upon what teachers do in their classrooms. Indeed, a substantial proportion of the regulation of teaching and learning has been devised without any clear thought as to how it might facilitate or constrain teaching and learning.

School reform usually involves some degree of adjustment to this regulatory apparatus, either by addition, deletion or reframing of the rules at one or more of the levels. An inspection of the regulatory framework may imply that only a minor refinement of the regulatory framework is required to put the reform into effect. Reformers usually want to change one part of the education system and are dismissive of the rest. They concentrate on the tip of the iceberg of rules and ignore the huge bulk of related rules which are not visible, but which, to extend the metaphor, are waiting below the surface to collide with the intentions of the reformers.

Notes

1   These books attempt to clarify the legal responsibilities of teachers and the kinds of litigation that might be brought against teachers for negligence or malpractice. A comparative, cross-national analysis is found in Birch and Richter, 1990; Birch, 1993.

2   The nomenclature for these positions varies among countries. In Australia, the political figure has the title of Minister for Education and the administrative head is known as the Director General. This separation of powers is common in countries with a Westminster tradition. There is no simple equivalence with the US where a state superintendent may be an elected official and where the administrative head of a state department may also be a member of the state cabinet. The equivalence is further disturbed by the powers given in the US to district boards

of governance and the district superintendents who are appointed by them. In Australia there is no such administrative layer.

3   Sometimes the responsibilities and functions of administering public education are splintered into separate pieces of legislation, for example, matters related to teacher registration may be contained in a separate statute. However, whether these functions are combined in a single piece of legislation or separated is largely a matter of administrative and legal convenience. The significant feature of the legislation is that, generally, all these functions are under the control of a member of cabinet.

4   Despite the lack of certainty about the capacity of officials to follow through on their stated intentions which immobilizes many in the education community, some individuals make shrewd political judgments based on their interpretations of the implications of policy statements and are able to position themselves favourably should changes eventuate. Because of this capacity to wield informal power, the formal status of policies cannot be ignored.

5   Needless to say, each of these management devices spawned more rules and guidelines. For a review of the introduction of corporate management in the Australian context see Considine, 1988.

6   Education department officials (public servants), teachers, support staff and cleaners and gardeners in most Australian states have separate awards and are covered by separate unions thereby complicating negotiations relating to workplace reform.

7   The current approach that is being adopted nationally is to produce curriculum frameworks which consist primarily of statements describing expected student learning outcomes (see for example, Education Department of Western Australia, 1994). Ostensibly, this approach ought to liberalize approaches to teaching since only the outcomes are fixed: teachers are nominally free to choose the 'method' of instruction that in their judgment will maximize the learning of the stated outcomes. However, the student outcomes approach implies that what is to be taught and how the content is to be taught are independent of each other. The atomistic breakdown of the curriculum into thousands of sections of content assembled under an outcomes rubric with clearly enunciated sequences of learning, and with outcomes tied to grade levels, constitutes a major constraint. I am not arguing the merit of this approach, rather I am questioning whether teaching is deregulated by the adoption of outcome statements unaccompanied by rules about how the outcomes are to be taught.

8   If something goes seriously wrong it is the Minister who is sued not the errant principal or teacher. However, teachers and principals can expect to be subject to disciplinary action if this occurs.

9   The reason given is that under the Education Act, only the Minister who can be held accountable because it is this office which is the legal entity.

10 Rampant rule making among managers is well-described in Gilbert, 1991.

11 For example, the state director of a unit established to introduce micro-economic reform by reducing the 'myriad of overlapping and conflicting statutory provisions' told me that his unit lacked 'teeth' and was reduced to a propagandizing role for government. In his autobiography Henry Bosch (1960), formally Chairman of the National Companies and Securities, described the opposition he faced in attempting to deregulate (or 'relax') auditing and accountancy rules. Most senior education officials whom I interviewed admitted that their systems of official rules were in an unsatisfactory state and indicated that they would eventually do something about it. However, they would not have wanted an external agency to do the job for them.

3   Regulation and Teaching

Despite the diversity of subject matter content, the identifiable forms of classroom activity are not great in number. The labels: 'seatwork', 'group discussion', 'teacher demonstration', and 'question-and-answer period' (which would include work 'at the board'), are sufficient to categorise most of the things that happen when class is in session. 'Audio-visual display,' 'testing session,' and 'games' might be added to the list, but in most elementary classrooms they occur rarely. (Jackson, 1968)

Introduction

In Chapter 2, I drew attention to one of the paradoxes of school education: despite the myriad official rules there are relatively few that direct teachers' classroom work. This is surprising given that the similarities among schools with respect to teaching practice are so striking that it seems as if most teachers are following the same set of rules. I attempt to explain this apparent paradox in terms of the nature of the relationship between regulations and teaching practice. I argue that inherent in the relationship between teaching and the rules which frame it, is a tendency to support the status quo which, ultimately, serves to undermine both diversity and reform.

The argument I am advancing in this book seeks to explain why rules can appear on the surface to maintain the predominant forms of teaching yet fail to deliver intended changes when they are manipulated in mandated reform. My explanation does not require me to refute commonly presented explanations in the research literature for the failure of 'top–down' reform, for example, the active resistance of teachers[1], and the inadequacy of resources.[2] I accept that in many cases these explanations of the failure of particular reforms will stand in their own right. However, they are not adequate explanations, by my account, of why standard patterns of school organization and teaching have endured in the face of concerted efforts to change them. I am positing a more general explanation.

I argue in this chapter that teaching practices occur within a regulatory context which functions like a shell; it surrounds teachers' work but lacks the capacity to intrude into it.[3] To extend the mollusc metaphor, the work of teachers is like a soft, muscular animal within the shell; it has many qualities which can be observed but which are more difficult to define than those of the outer shell. It is only by considering the way in which the inner and outer parts support each other that it is possible to understand the way the organism as a whole maintains its viability.

Established Teaching Practices

School teaching is a relatively private occupation. Many teachers spend most of their professional lives behind closed doors, out of sight of colleagues and rarely exposed to professional surveillance. Despite this, few teachers develop approaches which differ remarkably from their colleagues.

On a larger institutional scale, the same could be said of school organizational formats. The day is divided up into periods, the curriculum into subjects, the instructional content into lessons, the students into class groups and the buildings into classrooms, with all of these facets patterned by a school timetable. This is true of school organization in most western countries. Though there are exceptions to this general form of administration, in most school systems the exceptions are usually the result of necessity brought about by small student enrolments or some other administrative exigency. Occasionally, there are deviations that have been inspired by educational thinking, for example, my earlier reference to open plan schools, but these deviations are usually short-lived. Prevailing patterns appear to have endured for most of the century. This is even the case where concerted efforts have been made to change these patterns.

Durability of itself is not necessarily a negative feature of school organization and pedagogy. However, durability in conjunction with uniformity is a concern since this combination suggests an incapacity to adapt. Yet, paradoxically, teachers have shown a surprising willingness to try innovative teaching methods. Participation in trials and experiments is regarded as a professional virtue. Professional development, in which experts promote the latest curriculum materials and instructional practices, are part of the professional landscape. The problem is that the new approaches come and go, leaving behind little apparent residual benefit or, even, evidence that they ever took place.

Researchers who have examined the phenomena of uniformity of forms of teaching and their enduring nature usually find them easier to illustrate than explain (see Sirotnik, 1983; Goodlad, 1984; Cuban, 1984; Cuban, 1990; Cohen and Grant, 1993; Tyack and Cuban, 1995).[4] The question that I will now address is whether the regularities of school organization and pedagogy can be explained by the formal and informal rules that operate in schools and school systems. There are several different ways of approaching this question.

Frames

Urban Dahllof (1971) and Ulf Lundgren (1972) developed the idea that there are practical limits to what teachers can do.[5] These practical limits, which they called 'frame factors', include such things as the physical environment in which lessons take place, the textbooks and materials used for instruction, syllabus and assessment requirements and the time available. Although these factors may not lead teachers to adopt particular approaches they circumscribe or place conditions on teachers' work. These factors constitute a framework from which it is almost impossible for a teacher to move beyond. Dahllof and Lundgren compared their notion of external, practical limits to the conditions which teachers can control themselves. These conditions, which they referred to as 'process factors', interact with the external limits to create particular approaches to teaching.

Lundgren illustrates his theory with observations of verbal interaction in a classroom where there is a limited amount of time to cover extensive or difficult subject matter. In this situation, the teacher homogenizes the class into groups of pupils in order to reduce the complexity of 'pedagogic management'. The teacher then uses the progress of one of these groups within the class to determine when to move on to the next topic of content. Lundgren calls this group the 'steering group'. Because of the limitations of one of the external factors, that is, time, verbal interactions between the teacher and the class are kept to the bare minimum required by the steering group.

> Tight framing forced the instructor to 'pilot' the pupils through a problem without the pupils obtaining the prerequisite knowledge to solve that problem . . . What the pupil learns is as much knowledge of his own capacity to understand 'arithmetic-as-a-subject-in-school' as arithmetic itself. In this process identities are created: pupils learn something about themselves, about mental work, and about their own capacity to carry out this work. (Lundgren, 1983, p. 152)

Dahllof and Lundgren's frames, for example, time and requirements to cover curriculum content, are embedded in the regulatory framework which surrounds the work of teachers. Some of the rules that constitute the regulatory framework governing the use of time may be set locally by the principal and staff whereas others may be set by the district or state office. Collectively they frame the teaching. Although these frames cannot direct teachers to teach in a particular way, they do make it more likely that they will teach using established methods.

Instructional Guidance

David Cohen and James Spillane (1992) also explore the relationship between teaching practice and external regulatory influences. Rather than using the concept of outside factors framing practice they introduce the concept of 'instructional guidance' which is based on the idea that teaching and learning can be shaped by policies which support good practice. They defined five classes of 'instruments' that can provide instructional guidance. These are:

1 instructional frameworks;
2 instructional materials;
3 assessments of student performance;
4 oversight of instruction; and
5 requirements for teacher education and licensing.

Thus, school syllabuses, textbooks, assessment and examination procedures, forms of school and teacher inspection, and the credentials that teachers are required to possess — each an example of one of the five instruments of instructional guidance — circumscribe what teachers do. Usually, the policies and regulations which shape the form of each instrument are controlled by officials from outside the school.

The problem that Cohen and Spillane draw attention to is that instructional guidance may lack both consistency and focus; the instruments that they describe often work at cross purposes with each other even though, in theory, the instruments are under the control of authorities in some part of the overall education system. This has unfortunate consequences for teaching, they write.

> Many teachers and students are aware of different sorts of advice, but few are keenly aware of most of it. Many know that most guidance is either weakly supported or contradicted by other advice and that much can safely be ignored. The din of diverse, often inconsistent, and generally weak guidance opens considerable latitude to those who work within it. (Cohen and Spillane, 1992, p. 22)

Cohen and Spillane conclude that this latitude enables teachers to take the line of least resistance which is to rely on instructional habits that have been well established. In the absence of strong instructional guidance capable of supporting alternative pedagogies, most teachers fall back on familiar and comfortable practices. To put their conclusion in terms of my shell metaphor, Cohen and Spillane suggest that changes to pedagogy could be expected if the regulatory shell could be penetrated or its overall dimensions altered.

'Good' Teaching Practice

Possibly because there is no universally agreed construction of best practice for teaching, rules requiring particular approaches to teaching are rarely specified. Even if there were agreement about best practice, it would most likely incorporate personal qualities such as those of commitment, ingenuity and perceptiveness which cannot be mandated. Although such human virtues may be too illusive to prescribe by regulation, there is scope for investigating which attributes of teachers' work might be supported by external structures.

Richard Elmore (1995) defines best practice in terms of five principles drawn from current research.[6] In summary form they are:

1 the object of teaching is to nurture understanding;
2 understanding occurs in the context of specific bodies of knowledge;
3 understanding requires the development of basic and higher order skills simultaneously;
4 learners differ substantially in the experience, the cognitive predispositions, and the competencies they bring to the specific bodies of knowledge; and
5 learning is a social as well as an individual process.

Elmore then argues that the process of teaching and learning is organized around a limited number of regularities which are not necessarily conducive to the principles of best practice; he cites four such regularities:

1 the grouping of students for instruction;
2 the definition of teachers' work *vis-à-vis* groups of students;
3 the allocation of time for the coverage of bodies of content; and
4 the assessment of students' progress.

Elmore points out inconsistencies between what is known about the principles of best practice and the regularities of teaching context. He argues that the structures have become fixed because they help people to manage the demands and uncertainties of mass education not because they support good teaching practice. His key point is that the principles of good practice should define the appropriate structures rather than the other way around; the tail ought not be wagging the dog. School restructuring needs to be guided by a consensus on preferred practice. This position implies that the school is the starting point for reform and that plans being developed by school staff members to improve teaching and learning should proceed until they bump into the regulatory shell that frames what they can do. When this happens they should seek to remove the obstruction. Such arguments assume the cooperation of those who control the regulations that hold the structures in place.

The Nature of the Relationships Between Regulation and Teaching

It is difficult to predict the consequences on teaching of tightening or loosening the controls since the relationships are not direct but are more of the nature of the interconnections in a web. For example, regulating content by imposing curriculum and assessment frameworks constrains how time is used during instruction. Conversely, regulating the time limits of instruction may shape the sequencing of content and the amount of content covered. Regulating time *and* content considerably narrows the teacher's instructional options and, as Lundgren has illustrated, can have profound consequences on the teacher's pedagogy and what students learn.

Edgar Jenkins (1995) provides an example of the indirect links between regulation and teaching. He describes how the science component of the national curriculum in England and Wales, defined by an official regulation, required all teachers in grant-maintained schools to teach and assess what the regulation referred to as 'scientific investigation', that is, practical, hands on applications of scientific method. Jenkins quotes a survey of science teachers in which it was reported that many respondents felt very positive about the notion of scientific investigations, believing that they lay at the heart of all good science education. Presumably, the authors of the regulation also valued scientific investigation given the content of the ordinance.

Despite the apparent agreement about the value of scientific investigation, Jenkins argued that in many schools the mandate led to increased use of worksheets and whole-class instruction, which was not the intended outcome. He explains this in terms of the failure of top–down reform towards which there is sustained and organized opposition. According to Jenkins, individual science teachers created their own policies in response to the central government initiative. Whether this was the result of passive resistance or merely being overwhelmed by the scale of the reforms, science teachers appeared to be acting against their professional interests. His study suggests that the relationship between the particular regulation and the science teachers' work was not a direct one even when, nominally, there was agreement on what constitutes good science teaching.

Another example of an attempt to influence teachers' work by adjusting the requirements made of them is provided by Penelope Peterson, Sarah McCarthey and Richard Elmore (1996) who conducted case studies of three schools undergoing restructuring. They found that changing school structures did not make much difference to the pedagogy of the teachers. They argue that structural change often distracts from the more fundamental problem of changing teaching practice. For example, one of the structural changes, the introduction of team meetings, largely provided teachers with an opportunity to discuss routine matters rather than new ideas about teaching and learning. In the view of Peterson and her colleagues, teacher beliefs were more important than structures. This being so, they concluded that appropriate recruitment and selection procedures were needed in order to assemble and maintain a school staff able to act on the shared beliefs.

I agree with Peterson and her colleagues that a shared understanding about what needs to change and a joint commitment to put new ideas into effect are usually central to the successful implementation of just about any school reform. However, the analysis of Peterson and her colleagues could be construed not so much as evidence of the relative unimportance of structural change than as an illustration of the insufficiency of it in the absence of other kinds of change. Restructuring that arbitrarily modifies some structures and not others cannot be expected to succeed in the long run. If achieving the degree of understanding and commitment necessary to sustain school reform is contingent on recruitment and selection procedures, the structures which govern these procedures cannot be ignored. The problem is that such structures are seldom self-evident. Even when evident, the structures are thought to be beyond the control of school staffs. This leads them to concentrate their reform effort on the factors that are under their control — those within the shell.

Work Organization

Although education academics may seek to understand the framework which surrounds teaching in terms of questions about how these impede, support or shape good practice, the actual decisions about how the existing framework will be maintained or adjusted occur within collective bargaining processes. In this context, the language of Dahllof and Lundgren's frame factor theory and Cohen and Spillane's instructional guidance are replaced by representations of improvements or reductions in working conditions and productivity. In this arena, the shell which surrounds teaching and learning is 'work organization'.

Work organization encompasses a wider set of structures and functions than is usually associated with school organization and teaching. To understand why teachers teach the way they do it is necessary to understand what else they do, and to whom they relate when they make decisions about their pedagogy. On the surface, the work organization-determined regularities of schooling may appear to be too far removed from teaching and learning itself to have an impact because they are often two or three steps removed. However, these parameters have a covert role in extending or limiting teacher discretion.

Consider the obvious parameter of class size. The construct of a class is central to the thinking, not only of those who work in schools, but also officials who are given responsibility for managing the school system. School authorities have built vast, rule-governed administrative systems around assumptions that students will be grouped in classes of a certain size, under the care of a teacher for certain blocks of time during the school day, and engaged in learning particular bodies of discipline or content knowledge. Their own administrative systems have become wholly dependent on the notion. Recruitment, appointment, transfer and promotion systems operate with such systems in mind.

Administrators found it easier to support pedagogy which did not require the collaboration of several classes of students or several teachers: cross-memberships are difficult to achieve without the imposition of complicated timetables and networks of responsibility. Though there may not exist any regulation prohibiting such activities as collaboration between teachers, or sharing of responsibilities for students, the regulation of class-size maxima and the need of administrators to minimize complexity and uncertainty, have a domino effect, progressively and cumulatively making it more and more difficult for teachers to depart from the orthodoxy of one teacher per fixed number of students.

Education departments have not been able to disregard the idea of class size. Parents, schooled in these systems, have come to expect that their children will be taught under familiar conditions and look askance at deviations. Although education departments do not like being in this bind, they have allowed governments and the wider public to interpret class size as an index of quality.

Teacher unions have also played a key role in maintaining the rule system that defines teachers' work organization. Traditionally, their interest has been in safeguarding and, where possible, improving their members' working conditions. The most simple and salient index of such improvement has been average class size. Smaller classes supposedly lead to less work for teachers and better learning conditions for students. Hence, unions have applied pressure on governments to target class size reductions in their budgets and used average class size as a benchmark of quality, notwithstanding the fact that across-the-board reductions in class size require a substantial addition to the budget or a diversion of funds from some other area. Where these conditions have been stipulated in industrial agreements between unions and teacher employers they provide a kind of ratchet; levering up one notch at a time is considered progress while releasing the pressure is seen to result in an inevitable downward slide.

Thus, the allocation of students into classes is the dominant, though by no means only, facet of work organization. The division of the school day into blocks of time called 'periods', or the organization of groups of students into 'classes' are obvious aspects of work organization which frame the work environment and support or inhibit particular forms of teaching. School hours are usually fixed in regulation, also. So is the length of the school year. The division of work between teachers, administrative staff and aides is usually specified in duty statements and follows long-held conventions. The examinations at the end of schooling and the structure of the content are usually governed by formal rules. The rate of progress of students through school is not always mandated by particular regulations though, in practice, the prerequisite learning expected of students in grade levels maintains students in age or grade cohorts.

Conclusion

In general, teaching *per se* is not regulated though teachers are not free to do as they wish. This is because the conditions which *frame* teaching are highly regulated. Teachers, therefore, work within a regulatory 'shell' that both protects and constrains what they do. They can be creative within it but it becomes harder for them to change their work practices if the changes are contingent upon teachers contravening the regulations layered around them.

This carapace of regulation, at least partially, accounts for the uniformity and durability of particular forms of pedagogy and school organization. It is a mistake to regard the regularities as exclusively caused by a set of structures that exist outside the realm of human agency. The current focus on restructuring *schools* deflects attention from the regulations that hold many of the structures in place.

Changing work organization regulations would change the shape of the shell and consequently the room to move within it. By systematically regulating the policy parameters that define the shell, and by enforcing the regulations, teachers might change what they routinely do but it is difficult to predict precisely how pedagogy would change since the various parameters are highly interactive and the effects deceptively subtle.

In this chapter, I have argued that changing rules about teachers' work seldom seems to produce the *intended* changes in practice. However, it is a mistake to attribute a failure to demonstrate intended changes or direct relationships between particular rules to the irrelevance of the regulatory framework as a whole. As I will show in later chapters, in its entirety the regulatory framework has a significant impact on the powers teachers are able to exercise in performing their roles. It is the whole which draws teachers back to a traditional classroom pedagogy with which they and their students are familiar. This whole is extraordinarily complex and allows many countervailing forces to work within it.

Notes

1   See, for example, Rosenholtz (1988) who argues that teachers actively seek control of their work and use their technical knowledge to acquire considerable task autonomy. Teachers do not like taking orders from their bureaucratic superiors and are willing to test the limits of their professional jurisdiction. The resistance can be quite passive. Teachers develop compliance behaviours that enable them to meet the letter of the law when required, but to ignore the spirit when they choose; without such a capacity schools would have suffered an institutional collapse after hopping from one reform foot to the other. The resistance can also be quite overt. Teacher unions have provided teachers with the means of legitimate resistance, particularly to reforms initiated by the employers. In this respect schools are no different from other workplaces which have an active union presence. See also Gitlin and Margonis, 1995 who argue that teacher resistance to reform may be due to a proper assessment that various preconditions, such as the restructuring of teachers' work, must be met in order for the reform to work. The way in which teacher resistance can be played out has been well documented in the case studies of McNeil, 1988.

2   The empirical research evidence relating to the claim that improvement in student learning is contingent on extra resources is equivocal and extensive. The recent debate in *Educational Researcher* between Eric Hanushek and Larry Hedges is indicative. See the May 1994 issue of *Educational Researcher* in which Hanushek's contention that there is no strong or systematic relationship between school expenditures and student performance is challenged by Hedges and colleagues.

3   Lee Shulman (1983) employs a similar metaphor in which he likens the environment within which teachers work to a 'shell within which the kernel of professional

judgment and decision making can function comfortably.' The shell, according to
Shulman has a protective function, allowing teachers to deal with unpredictable
complexities created, in part, by external mandates. The art of good educational
policy making is to determine the contour of the shell and the size of the 'irredu-
cible kernel' in such a way that the State is able to meet its obligations and teachers
able to exercise their professional judgment adequately.

4 Most of the documentation and argument is drawn from schools in the United States
though the descriptions seem stereotypical of school teaching in Australia.

5 The response to Dahllof and Lundgren's frame factor theory was not extensive
beyond Europe.

6 The particular construction of best practice formulated by Elmore is not central to
his argument or mine.

4   School Reform as Re-regulation

But the point about rules, as Wittgenstein recognized and great artists might confirm, is that there are ways of following them which end up transforming them — that it is not just a choice between being inexorably coerced by them on the one hand, or being in a state of permanent anarchy on the other. (Eagleton, 1995)

Introduction

Although there is a voluminous literature on school reform not much of it examines the regulatory aspects. The statutes and regulations, which were essential for many reforms to proceed, have been of peripheral interest to researchers. Most contemporary reform is based on quite distinctive regulatory strategies: the imposition and adoption of new rules, exemption from official rules, or a combination of both. Further, as I have illustrated in Chapter 2, the new statutes that underpin the reforms usually precipitate a landslide of subsidiary rules which somehow have to be meshed with massive collectivities of existing rules. Rule changes are an integral part of reform attempts.

In this chapter, I have two purposes. The first purpose is to illustrate the omissions on the part of reform reviewers many of whom do not refer to the rules in place before a reform is introduced or the subsidiary rules which follow it. These rules are left in the background; their existence and effect are taken for granted.

My second purpose is to locate my own argument within the context of contemporary reviews of school reform. Because good, general syntheses of the research on school reform already exist, I will focus specifically on some key aspects of this literature pertaining to the regulatory frameworks in which the reforms are embedded.[1]

The Regulatory Components of Reform

From my perspective, many of the studies of reforms which entail legislative intervention, often referred to as top–down reforms, are problematic. It is common for reviewers to treat statutes as 'inert' directives which have only one meaning that has been ascribed to it by legislators. There is little acknowledgment of the different meanings for people in different contexts and roles, or if there is, these different meanings tend not to be described with sufficient detail or clarity to encourage analysis of the impact of these differences in viewpoint. Studies of mandated reform tend to adopt a macro perspective which excludes idiosyncrasy and detail, even though, finally, whether a reform is adopted or not may depend upon micro adjustments to existing protocols and rules.

In seeking to draw attention to relationships between reform and rule changes, I differentiate between reforms which have been based on new rules being added and those which purport to take rules away. The latter group includes reforms which are represented as forms of de-regulation and those which provide a basis for individual schools to gain exemption from rules. The National Schools Project sits within this last group. I also cite studies which seek to analyse the dynamics of change processes.

Adding Rules

Legislatures worldwide have been actively engaged in generating new regulations pertaining to education, believing that only by their forceful intervention can the problems confronting school systems be alleviated (see Fuhrman *et al.*, 1988).[2] This has occurred notably in the US and Britain.

Susan Fuhrman (1994) has given an account of the general phenomenon of regulatory additions in the US. She reports that between 1980 and 1986, more than a thousand pieces of legislation regarding teacher certification and compensation were introduced in state legislatures. The various statutes required the imposition, in turn, of further, more fine-grained regulations and guidelines for school districts. There was so much regulatory activity, according to Fuhrman, that policies were developed which were quite contradictory in their consequences; districts were obliged to sort out the ambiguity as best they could. Although Fuhrman traces various structural changes in districts and schools directly to these new statutes, she is qualified in her assessment of the impact on teaching and learning of the regulatory reforms introduced during this period.

In another example of a US study, Allan Odden and David Marsh (1988) describe the outcome of Californian omnibus legislation, SB 813, which contained more than eighty provisions including new requirements for high school graduation, new criteria for textbook selection and homework policies. In general, Odden and Marsh regard the legislation as a success since most of the schools in the sample they studied adopted the provisions. However, the researchers consider this legislation as foundational and recognize that there is a need for a more complex reform agenda; they comment that it was difficult for schools engaged in the implementation of SB 813 to change the nature of the teaching that took place or the academic curriculum, particularly the teaching and learning of skills such as problem solving and critical thinking.

In Britain, the Education Reform Act of 1988 is an example of comprehensive and complex new legislation designed to restructure the public education system.[3] The Act, in Rosalind Levacic's terms (1995), established the structure of the market within which schools may compete, specified the output to be produced by schools and specified the standards for the inputs into schooling. In practical terms, it established grant-maintained schools that would operate outside the control of the Local Education Authorities and set up national curriculum and assessment frameworks that all schools would be subject to.

The translation of the Education Reform Act into practice has not been straightforward and it has required review and modification, however, there is evidence that it has had an impact in classrooms, particularly in regard to curriculum content and assessment. Generally, this is represented by researchers in negative terms which is not surprising given the extent of opposition to the changes among the education community. Teachers did not want to work within national frameworks that were to be applied in a market-driven environment characterized by open enrolment, local management of schools, testing and publication of results and changes in the powers of school governing bodies.

Stephen Ball (1994) represents teachers' work as becoming increasingly over-determined and over-regulated as a result of the new legislation. This has occurred through a 'codification' of tasks required of teachers when they adopt the programs of study and the attainment targets specified by the national curriculum framework. Their adoption in turn narrows the range of teaching approaches; a particular program of study, for example, might 'dictate' certain forms of student grouping. The net result is increased standardization and normalization of established classroom practice. This account is consistent with that of Edgar Jenkins (1995) who describes the responses of science teachers to the same set of changes.

These authors, Fuhrman, Odden and Marsh, Ball and Jenkins, claim little evidence of tangible improvements in teaching and learning in schools as a result of major new legislation. Two of them, Ball and Jenkins, in fact claim that a deterioration in teaching and learning occurred because of the greater centralized control exercised over teachers' work resulting from the new legislation in England.

'De-regulation'

A major thrust in school reform has come from a view that bureaucracies constrain and control schools to the detriment of their teaching and learning goals. These days, hardly anyone has a good word to say for bureaucracy. Its supposed advantages of efficiency and adaptability now seem overstated. In many people's minds, the word 'bureaucracy' means mindless attention to rules or, even worse, a determination on the part of officials to block all initiative.[4] Not surprisingly, there are plenty of critics of bureaucratic forms of management in education.[5]

Attempts to 'de-bureaucratize' school systems have taken various forms.[6] School-based management, charter schools and arrangements to enable schools to be exempted from regulations are variations of a kind: experiments designed to release schools from some of the central controls that have traditionally governed schools.

Reform initiatives which go under the banner of school-based management purport to extend the authority of individual schools to make (or abolish) their own rules. Within this broad definition, various forms of authority may be devolved to varying degrees. Devolved powers may relate to administrative functions or school governance or both. At one end of the continuum, locally managed schools may acquire many of the attributes of independent, privately run schools; at the other end of the continuum, they may be required to do some of the mundane administrative work previously undertaken on their behalf by bureaucrats, possibly without ever having been consulted about the redistribution of work.

In the US, increased school-based management has occurred through the creation of Charter schools. These schools can be established under legislation which enables a charter-granting authority, usually a state government, district or university, to make a formal agreement with a consortium of individuals seeking to establish a school. The agreement outlines the terms on which government instrumentalities will provide funds for a school. The extent to which schools are freed from regulatory restraints varies as Priscilla Wohlstetter, Richard Wenning and Kerri Briggs (1995) point out.

In the state of Michigan, for example, charter schools must employ certified teachers, open their enrolments to any student who applies, operate within the framework of the Michigan Core Curriculum, follow the regulations that apply to public schools generally, not exceed per capita funding allocations to public schools and may not charge tuition fees. Subject to these constraints they may select their own staff, establish their own internal governance structure, produce school budgets and plans and develop their own ethos (Central Michigan University, 1996).

Wohlstetter and her associates conclude from their analysis of events in eleven states in the US that although policy makers want schools to be autonomous they are reluctant to exempt them from district and state regulations. The charter schools could restructure internally but whatever they did had to meet state and district regulations and reporting requirements. In their view charter schools may not have been given sufficient autonomy to make a real difference in performance.

One radical reform effort, employing the rubric of charter schools, has sought to 'break the mould' of established schooling completely. Under the auspices of the New American Schools Development Corporation, a non-profit, business backed organization was established to advance the America 2000 reforms of President Bush.

The New American Schools Development Corporation funded eleven design teams to work with communities after receiving nearly 700 applications. One such community was Bensenville, Illinois, a community of about 17,000 persons which won a grant for $1.25 million to design a school. The core idea incorporated in the Bensenville proposal was to abandon the concept of a school as an institution.

Jeffrey Mirel was employed as a consultant by the Bensenville New American School (BNAS) project group to write a history of the project. In his case history, Mirel writes:

> As noted earlier, the proposal called for substantial changes in educational organisation, especially in regard to the times and locations of classes and other learning activities; in the nature and structure of the activities, particularly in terms of curriculum design, pedagogical strategies, and the use of technology; and in the form of educational assessment. Specifically, the BNAS leaders sought to radically redesign such traditional aspects of education as the starting and ending time of the school day, the length of the school year, the activities of teachers, even report cards. Because these changes threatened to overturn basic routines as well as expectations of parents and students about what constituted a 'real school,' they contributed to the controversy about the proposal. Indeed, even if issues about governance and the union had been resolved, serious questions would have remained about the dramatic educational changes in the BNAS program. (Mirel, 1994, p. 508)

Though widely praised, well funded and with the designers cognizant of contemporary 'best practice' in the educational change literature, the project failed after a year of planning. The challenges to traditional notions of school governance and to the conception of 'teacher' as distinct from non-certified specialists drawn from the community created deep divisions in both the professional education and Bensenville communities. This is a cautionary tale.

In Britain, the equivalent of charter schools in the US are grant-maintained schools which were introduced following the Education Reform Act 1988. The Act introduced elements of choice and competition enabling schools to opt out of the control of Local Education Authorities (LEAs) and operate as independent schools, known as grant-maintained schools.

Priscilla Wohlstetter (1994) reports that by early 1994 there were 694 such schools in England. Grant-maintained schools are expected to adopt the national curriculum and participate in the national assessment program. However, they are freed from the regulatory apparatus established for schools under the control of the LEAs. Wohlstetter, in comparing the grant-maintained schools in England with charter schools in the US comments on the more aggressive posture of the British Government in empowering grant-maintained schools. Although the *stated* intention was to shift power from the LEAs to the consumer, critics, such as Mike Feintuck, argue that the power shift has occurred in the other direction — from LEA to the central government, more particularly the Secretary of State for Education who has been able to make executive decisions without legal challenge. There is no clear cut evidence that the official objectives of the reform have been achieved.[7]

In Australia, reforms under the banner of self-management have been introduced in different forms in the various states commencing in the early

1980s. This was done with very little regulatory adjustment; the body of official regulations was left almost completely intact.[8] In state public education systems, schools are required to produce management plans, take responsibility for some of the budget items that had been centrally controlled, and set up school councils with limited powers. The whole initiative, though often represented as 'empowerment' by its proponents, rests on central management prerogative which means that central officials can continue to intervene in a school when they consider it appropriate. The powers of school staff members *vis-à-vis* their employers have changed very little. The research evidence regarding the impact of this approach on student learning is equivocal at best.[9]

Exemptions from Rules

Methods for exempting schools from rules identified as being an impediment to teaching and learning goals have been called 'waivers'. Although in the same family as strategies which seek to de-regulate school systems, waivers are a more circumscribed form of regulatory change. They have been used to exempt schools or districts from specific rules or collectivities of rules for specified purposes and lengths of time, the purpose being to enable schools to introduce innovations which would otherwise be prohibited. Waivers have also been used to reward high-performing schools.

The exemption of schools from rules is of particular interest because this process constitutes a kind of 'natural experiment' in which rules which are seen to be limiting school performance can be identified and the consequences of their abolition or suspension observed. This is particularly interesting when teachers are involved in this process.

A number of studies of waivers have been conducted in the United States by the Consortium for Policy Research in Education. Susan Fuhrman, Patricia Fry and Richard Elmore (1992) report the results of *South Carolina's Flexibility through Deregulation Program in* which schools were given 'blanket' exemptions from education regulations or, in some cases, from categories of regulations. As well, schools could apply for exemption on a rule-by-rule basis. For the 164 schools which sought blanket exemptions during 1990–2 some limits were maintained. For example, health and safety regulations could not be altered; minimum six hour day for students continued to be mandated; high school graduation course requirements remained in effect; teachers still required basic certification. The exemptions applied mostly to time use, class structure and staffing.

Over the two-year period, the 'deregulated' schools instituted various forms of restructuring including integrated studies, multi-age classrooms and more planning time for teachers, however, according to colleagues associated with the program about half the activities undertaken could have been implemented prior to the introduction of the waivers.[10]

A similar picture emerged from an evaluation by Fry, Fuhrman and Elmore (1992) of *Schools for the 21st Century Program in Washington State*. Schools were invited to submit proposals for school restructuring to a state task force which would allocate funding and additional time for staff development and project planning. Twenty-one projects were finally selected from the 135 proposals submitted. Only six of the twenty-one projects required regulatory exemptions. Following a second round of submissions, only eleven of the thirty-three projects selected required exemptions. The exemptions were intended to provide schools with more flexibility in the design of course offerings and to vary the time limits for the school day and school year.

The results of these 'natural experiments' have been interpreted to mean that teachers see little need for regulatory reform. On the face of it, they were given an opportunity to challenge the rules and in most cases the changes they sought to make required no regulatory adjustments. The National Schools Project was conceived with similar intentions in Australia and fits this mould.

The National Schools Project

The National Schools Project was constituted as large-scale action research and was established to find out what improvements to student learning could be achieved by varying patterns of work organization, particularly aspects prohibited by regulation or industrial agreement. A sample of schools from across the nation would become the 'instrument' of the inquiry. The number of pilot schools grew from ninety, in 1992, to 170 in 1993.

A significant design feature of the National Schools Project was that schools were not instructed to change anything in particular. Instead they were encouraged to re-examine their operation and design work practices that would promote better teaching and learning. Where they encountered a regulatory impediment the unions and employers undertook to waive the rule for at least the duration of the trial, the idea being that if the change introduced by a pilot school proved useful then the regulatory framework would be amended to allow other Australian schools to benefit from the knowledge gained from the action research.

The schools participating in the Project did not generate 'earth-shattering' work organization proposals; there were few challenges to the status quo. In a survey of the Project schools in 1994, I found that only 8 per cent reported obtaining approval to operate outside the official rule system. Some of the exemptions that were granted appear relatively trivial — starting the school day fifteen minutes ahead of regulation time, re-scheduling professional development days so that they fell back-to-back, knocking out a wall between classrooms. Several were more challenging — redefining the duties of staff, teacher supervision of students on work placement during school holidays, the conversion of a school's allowance for teacher absences into regular teacher support time. These changes were not revolutionary or iconoclastic and, for the most part, they did not require exemptions. Yet within the regulatory framework there was considerable activity — James Ladwig *et al.*, 1994 describe 374 separate initiatives initiated by the 167 schools which they surveyed.

The responses of schools in the US and Australia have been strikingly similar. When staff in schools were offered the opportunity to work outside the rules most declined to take advantage of the opportunity. This response has been interpreted to mean that regulatory constraints are not an important aspect of school reform.

Analyses of Rule Changes

The principal interest of those investigating school reform had tended to lie in the question of *whether* a reform has worked which is understandable given the limited outcomes of many reforms. Because of this focus, there has been relatively little attention paid to the question of *how* reforms have worked. However, this latter question is crucial and must be answered before an understanding of the role of regulatory frameworks can be understood. In attempting to address this question, I have selected four studies which I consider to be pertinent.

The first of these studies is Richard Weatherley and Michael Lipsky's (1977) account of the Massachusetts Comprehensive Special Education Law which made 'local school districts responsible for the education of all handicapped persons aged three to twenty-one, regardless of the nature or severity of the handicap'. The new law required 'the greatest possible integration of handicapped children into regular class settings' (op.cit., p. 174). The official regulations that accompanied the Law specified what had to be done but did not specify how the implementation should be conducted.

The reform had potentially huge financial and administrative consequences and there were fears (that later proved groundless) of large numbers of handicapped children being dumped in regular schools. Districts were given a two-year planning time.

Weatherley and Lipsky studied the processes of identification, referral, assessment and the development of educational plans for the children with special needs in three school systems. They interviewed officials, attended meetings and examined relevant documents, including the records of all the children evaluated in relation to their special needs. Case studies were also conducted in seven schools drawn from the three school systems. Teachers from these schools were interviewed with respect to what happened to the children following their evaluation and the development of their educational plans. The evidence indicated that the objectives of the reform were not being achieved.

The failure of the special education reforms described by Weatherley and Lipsky can be explained in the usual way: inadequate funding, lack of professional training for classroom teachers, poor leadership and so on. Such shortcomings were evident. However, they construed the reform as the introduction of an innovation into continuing practice with its customary routine procedures, modification of goals and rationing of services so that the meaning of the reform was worked out at the school level, by the 'street-level bureaucrats', to use their term.

Weatherley and Lipsky gave their own insights into why powerful new laws are unable to penetrate practice. They write:

> However, in certain respects the new law, by dictating so much, actually dictated very little. Like police officers who are required to enforce so many regulations that they are effectively free to enforce the law selectively, or public-welfare workers who cannot master encyclopedic and constantly changing eligibility requirements and so operate with a much smaller set of regulations, special education personnel had to contrive their own adjustments to the multiple demands they encountered. (op.cit., p. 193)

The failure of the reform can also be explained in terms of the role of the street-level bureaucrats who were principally the teachers and school officials. In a confluence of formal and informal rules, this group constructed the reform in their own terms. The net result was that the law and its administrative regulations produced widely varying outcomes instead of the intended uniform set of procedures.

The Rand Change Agent Study is the second study I wish to cite. It is a classic reference in the literature on school change and was conducted over four years in eighteen states in the US, surveying nearly 300 school projects funded under Title III of the *1965 Elementary and Secondary Education Act* which was designed to support local innovation.

This study produced eight volumes of reports; Volume VIII, *Implementing and Sustaining Innovation*, written by Paul Berman and Milbrey McLaughlin for the Rand Corporation in 1978, is the best known. It was based on visits to twenty-nine project sites, observations of the projects in action and interviews with personnel at all levels.

The principal conclusion of the Rand Study was that successful innovations required the adaptation of the original ideas and the expected implementation procedures to the institutional setting. They found that the same innovation was implemented differently in each of the school districts they studied. Such adaptation was not necessarily indicative of mismanagement but could well mean that the innovation was taking root. Conversely, they argue, the apparently smooth and successful implementation without any adaptation might indicate that the innovation had been adopted but with minimal compliance. Further, they found that, 'Special projects focused on single issues or single inputs typically, by necessity, ignore the systemic and interconnected conditions that influence classroom practice' (see McLaughlin, 1990, p. 15).

Berman and McLaughlin describe a process of 'mutual adaptation' which is required in order for an innovation to fit into the 'embedded structures'. Although they made no reference to the role of regulatory frameworks in their work, clearly these can be seen as embedded structures. Mutual adaptation implies the adjustments required when new rules are introduced.

The third study I cite is an analysis by David Tyack and William Tobin (1994) which explains why the institutional forms of schooling have been so stable. They refer to the 'grammar' of schooling, the regular structures and rules that organize the work of instruction. Taking a historical perspective of schooling in America, they offer various explanations of why the structures and rules have been so hard to change and why, as a consequence, the institutional forms of schooling, such as the division of the curriculum into subjects or the classification of students and their allocation into classrooms, have persisted. Their conclusion is consistent with Berman and McLaughlin's notion of mutual adaptation: 'Reformers believe that their innovations will change schools but it is important to recognise that schools change reforms' (op.cit., p. 478).

A fourth study illustrating the implementation of the 'new' mathematics reform was undertaken by John Schwille and a team of colleagues (1983) from Michigan State University. In case studies of seven teachers, Schwille and his colleagues followed closely over the course of a year the content covered during mathematics instruction. They found, for example, substantial differences in the extent to which teachers followed the approved textbook. Even so, they concluded that the teachers were influenced in their selection of curriculum content by district policies. Schwille and colleagues predicted that teachers would even make changes that were inconsistent with their repertoire provided that the changes came from persons with perceived legal and expert authority and that they were assisted by adequate training and support.

Schwille *et al.* noted an emphasis on hierarchical control but also that the schools involved were too loosely coupled to the other levels of the school system for instructions issued by line managers to apply directly in classrooms with any consistency. Teachers exercised considerable discretion and made up their own minds about how closely to attend to the external policies. The teachers were 'political brokers, arbitrating between their own policies and the implied priorities of external policies' (op.cit., p. 387).

Teachers as Policy Brokers

Much of the reform effort has been initiated by central authorities, often involving regulatory change, either by prescribing new structures and procedures, or by authorizing schools to operate outside official regulations. The intention of this is to effect changes in teaching and learning in schools yet relatively little attention has been paid to the role of teachers in interpreting reform initiatives. However, if teachers are attributed greater agency than is customary, it is easy to take the next step and regard them as policy makers or policy brokers in their own right rather than passive recipients of the wisdom of others.

Dvora Yanow has likened the policy implementation process to a form of evolution. Once someone interprets a policy and acts on that interpretation they will communicate their interpretation to a second person who in turn interprets the previous interpretation of the original policy. A third person in the chain may encounter a policy so altered it can be viewed as a new policy. Yanow (1987) argues that the successive reinterpretations of regulations and policies are not random: they are responsive to the culture in which the implementation is taking place. Thus meaning develops and is communicated through a process of Chinese whispers. At a local level, teachers may judge a reform to be fully implemented when they have responded to the interpretation of the reform which is presented to them.[11] It may be no surprise that the teachers' actions have little connection to the original intentions of legislators.

This body of work on school reform, which examines the dynamics of regulatory reform, is the most helpful from my perspective. Some of the research is quite dated yet the implications that can be derived from it do not seem to have fully filtered into the thinking of present day researchers. Weatherley and Lipsky's study may have been confined to a single piece of legislation in one US state but there is reason to believe that what happened during the implementation of the Massachusetts Comprehensive Special Education Law would happen to a greater or lesser extent, with any complex piece of education legislation: the will of the regulators will never be transmitted with absolute fidelity across systems.

Conclusion

School reform commonly begins with regulatory change of some sort. The labels that researchers use as shorthand to describe the reforms — waivers, charter schools, school-based management, curriculum frameworks, and so on — indicate little about the nature or extent of the regulatory change. Syntheses of research which aggregate findings on the basis of these crude categories can be misleading because they confound or ignore important information about the regulatory context within which the reforms are expected to impact on teachers' work. Nevertheless, when examined in toto, this work suggests that regulatory reform seldom seems to deliver what was sought, irrespective of whether the reform involves adding official rules, deleting them or temporarily waiving them. Changing the official rules is not enough to guarantee the success of school reform.

Few studies have examined the micro-dynamics of official rules when gauging the impact of reform. This is due in part to the way in which reform is conceptualized — some sweeping, decisive interruption to the traditional way of doing things, usually as the result of some external force. Such a construction focuses the observer on certain kinds of features to the exclusion of others in much the same way that scientists prior to Darwin were unable to imagine that massive geological formations could be explained by the gradual accumulation of deposits. Thus, most studies of school reform pay little attention to how new regulations are integrated into larger systems of rules, mainly because the new regulations are plain for all to see whereas the remainder, the vast majority of the rules, have merged into the landscape. In order to understand why new rules are not observed it is necessary to examine them in conjunction with existing rules.

Notes

1 For example, Michael Fullan (1992) provides an excellent summary of the literature and various other scholars, including Susan Fuhrman and Richard Elmore, have recently edited collections of work that has concentrated on the impact of national, state and district reforms on school practice. However, they make only passing reference to the 'dynamics' of regulation from the perspective that I have adopted.
2 They write: 'What we have found is not a zero sum game but a net increase in governance. Every policymaker is making more policy' (p. 255). The growth in regulation through new legislation and policy is not confined to the education sector. Roderick Macdonald, with reference to the Canadian law, observes that the volume of regulation has increased, especially in recent years. ('Understanding regulation by regulation,' in Bernier and Lajoie, 1985; Birch and Richter, 1990) also note the growth of regulation and quote the view of Jurgen Habermas that the increasing volume of legal regulation is symptomatic of the 'colonization' of the private sphere whereby family, education and culture are being subjected to the rules of the political system.
3 I make a number of references to the Education Reform Act of 1988. However, because I have had no first-hand experience of living and working in England and Wales, either before or after the enactment, I have not made the Act a central example in my work. The Act clearly has had a massive impact on the school systems of England and Wales, and if the majority of reports are to be believed, a highly negative one. The reforms were opposed by the majority of the education establishment. Much of the academic writing is strongly charged with ideological argument, a reaction to the economic rationalism of the Thatcher Government and its successors. As the shock has worn off, and as the Government has belatedly begun to respond to the criticisms, it appears that the opposition is more conditional and measured than in the period immediately after the enactment. See, for example, Chitty and Simon, 1993. David Hargreaves (1994) argues that there have been positive outcomes of the reforms — the emergence of what he describes as a 'new' professionalism, for example — but the outcomes have been *unintentional.*
4 Typical of this sentiment is *From Red Tape to Results* authored by Vice-President Al Gore. Taking its cue from the private sector, the report calls for 'the elimination of regulatory overkill', 'cutting red tape', 'subjecting agency regulations to a waiver process', 'stripping away unnecessary layers of regulation that stifle innovation' and thereby radically improving the productivity of federal agencies. The 'Gore Report' (1993) unashamedly follows the line of Osborne and Gaebler, 1992. Not surprisingly, it spawned an education equivalent. Gerstner *et al.* who argue that to succeed, public schools must be 'de-regulated'. High standards will not be achieved by bureaucratic regulation. Regulations enforced by school districts, designed to limit 'worse-case' behaviour inhibit excellent behaviour as well (p. 52).

5   For example, Wise, 1990 argues that the pattern of increasing central control is to be avoided not because it represents a shift in power but because it reduces the responsiveness of schools to their clientele which, in turn, reduces the quality of education. This happens because the instruments of central control, for example, standardized tests, curriculum alignment across schools, and teacher evaluation, are too blunt. Wise argues for 'client centred' control rather than the abrogation of control to teachers. Chubb and Moe, 1990 are partly in agreement with Wise about the dangers of central, bureaucratic control. Central authorities breed bureaucracy and impede change, they assert. However, from their point of view, the solution is not simply to get the central bureaucrats off the back of enlightened school principals. The institutions that comprise the larger system are ineffectual and are in need of radical restructuring. School reform cannot afford to be left to the existing institutions since they are part of the problem of school reform. Chubb and Moe write: 'The Constitution and countless federal, state and local laws set out a structure of democratic authority — a massive, fragmented multi-level "organisation" blanketing the entire country — in which various offices have certain rights to impose decisions on the local schools.' (p. 39) Because of the widespread opportunities for non-compliance, education authorities 'bureaucratize' the implementation of policy and so generate more rules and constraints. Teacher unions do the same, motivated to protect their members' interests by specifying contracts and agreements in as much detail as possible. But Chubb and Moe's solution is not to enhance teacher autonomy but rather to strengthen *school* autonomy, requiring an altogether different course of action — eliminating the existing democratic forms of governance and opening the school system to market forces.

6   Louis and Miles (1990) examined through case studies the extent to which the relationship between school and district was bureaucratized, that is, formalized and governed by rules and regulations. They concluded that 'in general, high engagement is better for school improvement, coupled with fewer rules. In bureaucratic districts, school administrators must actively negotiate for latitude, or even 'go outside the rules' if effective school-based change is to take place.' (p. 182) Even in this book-length study there is little analysis of the rules *per se* which constrain the schools and the notion of bureaucracy is applied very generally.

7   Feintuck, 1994 argues that the model of competition has failed to offer any significant degree of empowerment to consumers. It has not enhanced the accountability of those who exercise power over schools, either and, finally, it has failed (so far) to produce an improvement in educational standards.

8   The limited devolution of power to local decision-making bodies can be regarded cynically as a deliberate misrepresentation of school-based management by officials reluctant to let go of the reins. There may, however, be legal constraints preventing officials from devolving powers. In such cases officials may opt to push ahead on a modest basis and hope that with increased public and political support, the legal obstacles may later be removed. Walker and Roder, 1993 cite the example of New York State where the State Board of Education is legally prohibited from delegating its power in a wide variety of areas including those that fall under the aegis of collective bargaining legislation. The same is true of public education in Australia.

9   On the basis of their review of the research evidence Ogawa and White (1994) are equivocal about the prospects of school-based management. At the time of their review the empirical evidence showed that the decentralization had not led to any

consistent improvement in student outcomes. Also, although school-based management had taken on a multitude of forms, in most cases it had provided schools with control over only a limited proportion of their total operating costs. More to the point of this review, the research quoted tended to ignore the specifics of the regulatory environment within which the schools were expected to exercise their delegated administrative responsibilities. For example, the few studies of the efficacy of the reform cited by Ogawa and White were conducted by looking for statistical differences on various outcome measures between a sample of schools involved in school-based management and a control sample of schools which were not. See Malen *et al.*, 1990.

Rosalind Levacic, in *Local Management of Schools*, reached a similar conclusion to Ogawa and White about the efficacy of school-based management. She quotes from a 1992 report of Her Majesty's Inspectorate which states that there is little evidence yet of local management of schools having any substantial impact on educational standards. Levacic argues that if local management is to improve school effectiveness then it must impact on the classroom. It may do this by enabling a more cost-effective deployment of a given quantity of resources or by stimulating those processes which are associated with school effectiveness and school improvement. If either of these intermediate kinds of changes are occurring, and Levacic thinks that they are beginning to occur, the effects on student learning are still too modest to be established statistically.

10   Another component of the South Carolina program was designed to support school innovation; during its first two years, of the seventy-one schools that were funded for the implementation of their innovations, only four received exemptions, all of which related to instructional time requirements. In a related component focusing on school dropouts, there were fifteen exemptions from thirty-two funded projects though many were applied on the same school site.

11   Measure A is decided on. The decision is followed by a directive and information on its implementation. At the local level the decision is converted into decision B, which is implemented. Decision B or measure is often already latent in the school's activities and solves a series of pre-existing problems. Measure or decision B is not the same as decision or measure A, but A makes B possible. As a result of B being implemented, decision A is seen in a positive light and the reform package of which A forms part comes to enjoy additional confidence, decision A is accompanied by a 'language' — nomenclature and new terminology. Decision or measure B is described in these terms. An evaluation of the implementation of A shows that this decision has been implemented. New decisions for change implicitly assume that measure A was effective. (p. 8)

This is not a universal pattern. Whether or not A is transformed into B depends on how tightly A has been framed. The more imprecise the expression of the goal of A the more likely it will be transformed at the local level. This explanation of how core ideas underpinning reforms are transformed is consistent with the results of an earlier study of my own (1992) *Chinese Whispers: The Transformation of Knowledge about Teaching*, Geelong: Deakin University Press. I examined how the central concepts emerging from research on the use of time — concepts such as 'academic learning time' and 'time on task' — were eventually translated into common sense terms by teachers who had participated in a professional development program designed to promote the research.

5   Rule Systems

Old rules, which have been really abolished, persist on an informal basis because they were cornerstones of complicated labour-saving routines which people have devoted a great deal of effort to mastering. They include, for example, the rules concerning cut-off numbers and their effect on the allocation of teaching appointments. Other older rules have been officially retained in Ordinances etc., even though they do not fit with the otherwise new system. These residual rules and routines can, if applied, preclude or impede the implementation of other routines, e.g. those necessary to decentralise forms of decision-making. Allowances for this co-existing, residual code of rules pushes reforms in a conservative direction. In fact, they guarantee that there will not be any systematic change. (Ahs, 1986)

Introduction

So far, I have provided a broad-brush description of the official rules that govern a public education system. In toto, this body of rules is extensive, multi-layered and covers many areas of content. In this chapter, I explain how people organize subsets of the multitude of official rules around topics of interest to them in order to make them more accessible and useful. I refer to these groupings of official rules as rule regimes.

I then outline evidence which suggest that most teachers and officials working in education systems have limited knowledge of the rule regimes which pertain to their areas of responsibility. This lack of knowledge is significant and leads to the question of how people make sense of official rules of which they have such limited knowledge. I address this question in this chapter.

My main contention in this chapter is that people develop constructions of the official rules which enable them to navigate their way through the regulated aspects of their work in a way which does not require them to have detailed or first-hand knowledge of the content of the formal regulatory framework. I explain the process by which this is done in terms of concepts of rule systems and social rule systems which, based on the work of Burns and Flam (1987), I have developed in regard to the implications for school reform.

Rule Regimes

In Chapter 2, I represented the corpus of official rules as a single, monolithic legal system. It can also be represented as a set of rule regimes which are collections of official rules pertaining to particular areas or topics.[1] These topics may be broad areas such as: instruction, curriculum, work organization, the powers of officials or disciplinary action. They can also be constructed around areas relating to specific duties or concerns, for example, timetabling, the role of the teacher aide or the length of the school year.

Rule regimes have legal foundations in specific pieces of legislation, subsidiary legislation, administrative instructions, formal policies and guidelines statements. They will also contain elements of cross-sector legislation and the common law. Some rule regimes may be documented for particular purposes, for example, when a major piece of new legislation has been enacted and officials seek to put it in context. They may also be identified by staff working in schools if they perceive a need, for example, if changes are contested on the grounds that they are outside the law.

To illustrate rule regimes I will describe two examples: promotion and tenure, and industrial negotiations. Promotion and tenure is a topic which is close to the hearts and minds of most career-oriented teachers some of whom monitor the formal rules in this area very closely. In Western Australia, the official rules relating to this field are derived principally from the Education Act Regulations, the Public Sector Management Act which sets whole-of-government rules, the Industrial Relations Act which details the requirements for employment contracts and tenure, and the Equal Opportunity Employment Act which addresses questions of discrimination. There may also be other forms of rules which have lesser legal status but which are formally articulated and documented, for example, the compendium of procedures published by the Education Department's personnel directorate. Rules relating to promotion and tenure which are derived from these separate and sometimes overlapping sources constitute a rule regime.

Industrial negotiations is another area where official rules are considered of great significance. These rules are complex, even arcane, and are derived from industrial law which delineates the rights of employers and employees and defines the procedures that must be followed to arbitrate disputes. The official rules in this area have not been developed with schools or even education systems in mind and knowledge of the industrial negotiations rule regime is generally limited to industrial officers. It is expected that their knowledge will be detailed and expert and will inform negotiating teams. I knew little about this rule regime until I became a member of a departmental negotiating team.

Rule regimes can overlap. Consider a situation where a management decision about promotion and tenure is challenged. This becomes an industrial matter and so at least two rule regimes come into play. If the complaint is related to another topic, for example, discrimination, then there may be more than two rule regimes pertaining to the situation. Even attempts to simplify and make the official rules more accessible may be to little avail once they are applied to real-life situations.

Knowledge of the Rules

As I have already said, I had little knowledge of industrial negotiations until I was plunged into them. I could have made the same comment about other rule regimes; for the most part I did not consult the formal rules unless there was the threat of some formal sanction arising from a breach of them. What I learned about the official rules was acquired on a need-to-know basis. I don't think my attitude differed greatly from the majority of my colleagues.

Most teachers have only a sketchy knowledge of the rules. In a written 'test' of their knowledge of the Education Act Regulations in which teachers in two schools were asked fourteen questions such as 'Under what circumstances may a child be excluded from school?', Ray Knight (1996) found that the teachers averaged about seven correct answers. The principals and deputy principals gained more correct answers than did classroom teachers, one of the principals answering thirteen out of fourteen questions correctly. Only five out of the thirty-seven staff members surveyed had ever referred to a printed copy of the Regulations; of these five, all of whom were principals or deputy principals, two had done so as part of postgraduate studies and three in order to resolve some uncertainty about their employment status.

Despite the lack of direct scrutiny of rule texts, half the teachers reported they believed they worked entirely within the boundaries defined by the official rules. However, as the proportion who had read the Regulations was small, it can be presumed that considerably more than half had not complied with Regulation 24 (1) which states that 'Every teacher shall make himself acquainted with the regulations and administrative instructions supplied to his school'!

Senior departmental officials in several Australian states also reported limited knowledge of regulatory texts. One commented that he had been a member of a departmental senior executive for twelve months and had had no need to look at either the Education Act and its Regulations or the teachers' award in that period of time. His counterpart in another state said: 'If you asked the average director of personnel in an education department what is in the teachers' award they wouldn't have a clue because it's not well known'. Somewhere, however, in union and departmental central offices there is a person or unit which scrutinizes the upper layers of the regulatory system. These officials, sometimes with legal backgrounds and qualifications, field the inquiries not only from teachers but also from senior management.[2]

A departmental senior officer explained how teachers find what they need to know about the regulations. 'At the moment they are still in the dependency model a bit. What tends to happen is that they ring the superintendent or the principal asks his supervisor or they ring me.'

This view of teachers asking someone else to interpret the official rules for them was supported by senior union officials whom I interviewed. Without exception, they expressed views that teachers were unaware of the official rules. One said:

I could write a guarantee that no school would have an up-to-date version of any of those [formal rules] and certainly I would suggest that 99 per cent of teachers haven't even looked at them, seen them, let alone flicked over a few pages. And the other thing that regulates their work is the Award. Now the Award is meant to be in schools and available, and yet only last year schools were actually given a copy of the Award for the first time. My own understanding is that most of them were locked in the filing cabinet.

A state teacher union president commented on the usual strategies teachers use when they want to find out about the official rules: 'We take thousands of information calls along the lines of 'The Education Department says I've got to do X', or 'What are my rights?'

It appears that most teachers and officials have only sketchy, first-hand knowledge of official rules and rely on others to provide 'expert' knowledge and to interpret them. To understand why rules can be highly significant yet at the same time people have such scant knowledge of them, it is necessary to consider the social meaning attributed to rules.

Rule Systems

It is no wonder teachers rarely refer directly to written collections of rules to clarify what they should do. Apparently straightforward actions can fall under the umbrella of multiple rule regimes of considerable complexity so that it is never clear what should be done. Under these circumstances teachers rely on their employer's or union's representatives to summarize the relevant regulations and advise them.

The questions teachers ask arise out of their work. They may not be framed in terms of rules even though the answers draw on rules. Examples of questions that are of interest to teachers are: Can I be forced to transfer if I don't want to? If I can, who has the power to enforce this? Whose influence should I be more concerned about: my principal's or my superintendent's? What role does the superintendent play? What do I need to do to obtain the superintendent's support? How can I impress a selection panel? There are many aspects to these kinds of questions; formal rules constitute just one aspect of the answers.

Teachers' questions can be answered in different ways. Some answers to teachers questions can be found in Acts and Regulations, although probably not on a first reading. Other answers require experiential knowledge of how 'the system' works. The teacher union uses its newspaper, conferences and branch networks to proselytize its point of view and so provide its answers to many of the questions which concern teachers. The Minister, delegates responsibility for answering teachers' questions to the head of the education department who in turn passes responsibility down the line.

The inconsistencies in the answers proffered, the Chinese whispers, create a state of flux within the politics, ideology and semantics of organizational life requiring teachers and officials to form their own simplified notions of the rules. This collection of memorized signposts needs to be constituted at a level of detail that teachers and officials can draw on in discussions or at meetings and provides a guidance system to enable them to steer their way around a range of problems and issues.

Social Rule Systems

Although individuals operate from different rule systems, there may also be an understanding about rule systems which is shared among a group. I refer to a rule system about which there is a shared understanding as a social rule system. Teachers' social rule systems are practical and functional. They organize their rule systems according to their everyday concerns and so are likely to pay little attention to the categories of rules described in the outline of the official rules.[3] Rather, social rule systems relate to such matters as managing disruptive student behaviour, how much time is allowed for non-teaching duties or the transfer rights of teachers. The social rule systems consist of interpretations of official rules massively supplemented with rules derived from local practice — how things are done in this school to the mutual satisfaction of teachers and administrative staff. Principals share much of this but also develop social rule systems about matters of particular concern to them, for example, school finance and school governance. Factored into their social rule systems are the expectations of their supervisors. Officials may employ quite different social rule systems from those of teachers and principals. They are more likely to share a view of the rules which recognizes its hierarchical layers and to see these as emblematic of the bureaucratic structures which ought to provide order to an education system.

To illustrate how a social rule system works, I will refer to one of the examples which I used earlier based on my own experience of industrial negotiations. One of my first discoveries when I began to participate in industrial negotiations was that there were unwritten protocols that I was expected to observe; these dictated what could be said formally and what was off the record, when to sound tough and when to seem conciliatory, what was a digression and what was central to the issue under discussion. It was implied that there were acceptable and unacceptable solutions to problems that were tied to fundamental union, employer or government principles and values. Sometimes the negotiators, teams of representatives of the employer, the union and, possibly, the government, behaved like characters in a pantomime and I expect that teachers, whom each side represented in its own way, would have been astonished to have observed what went on and how we behaved. I say 'we' because unfortunately I was drawn into it too.

The industrial negotiations rule regime was crucial to these activities but the problems that were being resolved drew upon a wider set of rules which included informal rules and tacit understandings. Though there may have been idiosyncratic differences between the states with respect to the climate and the procedures during negotiations, I felt confident after interviewing union and departmental officials in all Australian states that the industrial negotiations social rule system was fundamentally the same. It was as though the negotiators had all been to the same training institution and completed the same course on law, politics and the dramatic arts; anyone who transgressed these rules, as I know I must have at times, created tensions that were likely to exacerbate rather than solve problems.

According to Burns and Flam (1987), social rule systems do not occur on an *ad hoc* basis. Social rule systems are regulated by their users in ways which relate to the meaning and significance attributed to the systems themselves. These meanings are derived only in part from the official rules but are also subject to cultural, political and ideological influences.

Rule Systems and School Reform

There has been a tendency for those interested in changing schools to view official rules as either impediments or instruments of reform in their own right. Little attention has been paid to how people use rules and the effects of this on the reform process. However, it is useful to distinguish between the formal regulatory framework which is written on paper and the reference points which people carry around in their heads to help them to make sense of these rules. Doing so, raises a number of issues about what might be expected when reformers attempt to bring about improvement by a strategy such as the introduction of a new rule regime.

One issue, which is rarely considered, is that the kinds of rules which are either introduced or abolished as a result of reform initiatives are actually intended to change who needs to know about 'the rules'. Many reforms are based on a belief in the benefits of local decision-making or greater teacher professionalism. Consequently, they are introduced with the intention of challenging the rights of principals or officials to interpret rules for teachers. This means that the people teachers rely on to help them make sense of rules will be disadvantaged by the very rules they are being asked to interpret. It should not be surprising that the interpretations they provide undermine the status and practicability of the reforms.

Another factor which needs to be considered, is the effect social rule systems have on each other. The inconsistencies and contradictions between social rule systems are a fact of life. For example, the rule system regarding decision making in a school might not support the rule system about pedagogy. The former may centre power in the office of the principal and promote central, autocratic decision making whereas the school may be engaged in trying to make teaching more collaborative. It is quite common to find inconsistencies which work against each other. Contradictions can become evident within a school when people select contrary courses of action or when demands for resources exceed their availability. A school, therefore, can function with multiple social rule systems of varying degrees of consistency which, at times, are at cross purposes. It is possible, Max Weber (1978) observed, for individuals in the same social group to orient their actions to contradictory systems of order which may all be recognized as valid. These differences in orientation can become even more complicated when changes are introduced.

A third issue arises from the state of flux which results from competition between rule systems. Social rule systems are constantly changing. For example, one which was initially sympathetic to a reform may be later hostile towards it. People are continually forming and re-forming social rule systems even when the organizing principles and core structures are maintained over long periods of time. The process of rule system formation and re-formation is very much influenced by the particular contexts in which events take place and depends on the disposition of the people involved, for example, whether they are disposed to cooperate or engage in power struggles. Teachers may be initially receptive to a reform because they are dissatisfied with the status quo. Subsequently, they may be opposed to it because union officials have persuaded them that the reform will actually worsen their circumstances or increase their vulnerability in future.

Finally, social rule systems, by incorporating official and unofficial rules acquire a grey complexion; boundaries between authoritative directives and guidelines are blurred with local knowledge and custom. Policy statements can be accommodated easily within social rule systems because they are so organic. If they were not, then many aspects of schools and school systems would be even more constrained than they are now.

Conclusion

Changes to a regulatory framework are often introduced as a means of implementing changes in schools as though there were a direct relationship between statutes and the actions of teachers. Evidence suggests, however, that social rule systems operate in a way which buffers teachers from literal interpretations of the many, varied and often inconsistent regulatory texts which abound in education systems.

The interactions between regimes of official rules and social rule systems need to be taken into consideration when changes are proposed. It should not be expected that the introduction or removal of a rule regime, much less a single rule, has the power to cause teachers to behave, or stop behaving, in particular, specified ways. Governments may control rule regimes but they do not control social rule systems. Where there is an inconsistency between an official regulation and an established rule of a school, woven into a social rule system, it does not necessarily follow that legislative fiat will win out. Therefore, it may be helpful to conceive of school reform as a *reformation of a social rule system* (or in some cases, the reformation of a constellation of social rule systems).

Notes

1   I am using the term 'rule regime' slightly differently from Burns and Flam. They define rule regimes as particular kinds of social rule systems, namely those which are backed by social sanctions (p. 13). I use the term rule regime to mean the official regulations pertaining to a particular topic or function. They may or may not be fully integrated into a social rule system.

2   On a day-to-day basis, management of the official rules in the Education Department of Western Australia, which had a central office establishment of a thousand or so employees, was the responsibility of a single official during my time there. This official, who usually had a legal background, liaised with the Office of Crown Law where legislative amendments or changes to Regulations were drafted. While working in the Ontario Ministry of Education during 1978, I was surprised to find that a whole section, the Supervision and Legislation Branch, was devoted to the task of reviewing the Ontario education legislation and ensuring that school districts complied with the rules. I revisited the Ministry in 1996 and discovered that the section was now named the Legislation Branch, had been halved in number of staff and had a primarily legal focus. The supervision function had disappeared; the purview of the Branch did not extend to schools and districts. This was also true of the Michigan State Department of Education which I visited in 1996. The Department officials focused on the state-wide rules and were largely unaware of the rules established by districts and schools. The latter were not their business. Their job was to keep the upper layers of the official rules in order. Rule regimes and social rule systems that applied in schools were beyond their control.

3   I am employing the construct in general terms and form a sociological perspective. I am not proposing that the multiple rule systems constitute psychological schemata. Nor is my research purpose to map the various branches and nodes — the deep structure as it were. I am suggesting, however, that members may have a shared, general understanding of what particular rules mean, which rules need to be attended to, and which rules cluster in functional groups. I will take up this matter further in Chapter 8 when I discuss meta-rules.

6 Culture and Regulation

... I desired my liberty. It appeared that he understood me well enough, for
he shook his head by way of disapprobation, and held his hand in a posture
to show that I must be carried as a prisoner. However, he made other signs,
to let me understand that I should have meat and drink enough, and very
good treatment. Whereupon I once more thought of attempting to break my
bonds; but again, when I felt the smart of their arrows upon my face and
hands, which were all in blisters, and many of the darts still sticking in them,
and observing likewise that the number of my enemies increased, I gave
tokens to let them know that they might do with me what they pleased.
(Jonathon Swift from 'Gulliver's Travels')

Introduction

In the last chapter I argued that informal rules play an important part in
enabling teachers to make use of complex and internally contradictory systems
of official rules. However, informal rules also have a significance beyond this.
I begin this chapter by providing more elaborate descriptions of informal rules
and further developing explanations of how they operate.

An investigation of the role of informal rules begs questions about the
effects of school cultures on school reform. 'Culture' is often given as the most
important factor explaining a reform's success or failure. Such an explanation
is liable to ignore or understate the way that rules, particularly official rules,
function as elements of cultures.

I argue that to explain the limitations of reform solely in terms of culture
implies a dichotomy between culture and regulation which is difficult to substantiate. Teaching cultures and the regulatory framework of schools cannot
be so easily forced apart; culture can explain a great deal but not in terms that
assume it exists separate from the formal regulatory framework.

In this chapter, I seek to differentiate between the informal rules or norms
and a more broadly defined notion of culture in order to draw attention to the
role formal rules play in regard to each of these. In doing so I use the National
Schools Project as an example of a reform attempt which led many to conclude that change can only be achieved through adjustments to teaching cultures. I outline the argument that has been used to support this claim and
challenge the assumptions on which it is built.

Informal Rules

If you were a visitor, an outsider unfamiliar with the operation of schools, you might be led by the principal from his office (principals have nearly always been males) around the school and unless you happened to visit on a bad day, or it was recess time, you would be struck by the orderliness and the industry of the place. It would seem that everything is running according to expectations. These expectations are standard operating procedures reflecting the way things are done 'in this place' and constitute informal rules, many of which are rarely, if ever, codified or given an official status. Generally, they are learnt by watching others and from the disapproval which is directed at those who fail to understand their importance.

There is an extensive literature in sociology and social psychology on informal rules, often referred to as 'norms'.[1] The informal rules do not have to have a foundation in 'fact' to take effect. The more irrational the rules, that is, the more obscure their origins and explicit purpose, the harder they are to change. As informal rules emerge over time they become increasingly implicit and complex. They also carry more authority. While life runs more or less smoothly from day to day, very few doubt the validity of the existing norms and very few challenge their authority. Joseph Gusfield puts it this way:

> The most subtle forms of social control are those we least recognize as such precisely because the categories of understanding and meaning provide so powerful a constraint to what we experience and how we think about that experience, they prevent awareness of alternative ways of conceiving events and processes. Because they lead us to 'see' the accustomed forms as the only reality they minimize and obscure the possible conflicts and the volitionary decisions that have helped construct that 'reality'. (Gusfield, 1981, p. 28)

A colleague described to me an example of an informal rule she became aware of after visiting, as an adult, a high-fee paying school for girls she had attended as a student. She was struck by the uniformity with which everyone spoke softly. Staff and students alike all listened to each other; they spoke in whispers which were always heard. It was as though there was a rule which was being upheld by everything that happened in the school: 'It is important not to be noisy here.' This rule was not displayed on a notice board or even by teachers reprimanding students for not upholding the rule. The expectation had been established that being noisy was not an option available to the members of this community.

This is just one example of many unspoken rules which can be implied by observing behaviour. Other examples of such rules are: 'It is important to do what you are told here,' or, 'Do what everyone else is doing.' Either of these rules could become more complex in their application, for example, 'It doesn't matter what you do as long as you do what you are told,' or, 'Do what everyone else is doing and be careful not to draw attention to yourself'. If both these rules operated in the one school they might interact, for example, 'If you are told to do something that no-one else is doing, then you must have made a mistake.'

There are also informal rules of this kind which teachers might apply but which are not significant for other members of the school community. An example of one such rule is: 'Don't presume to have any interest in what other teachers are doing or expect that any other teacher will be interested in what you are doing'. An extension of this might then be: 'If other teachers show interest in what you are doing then you can presume that they want something from you or that they disapprove of your teaching.' This could then lead to a rule: 'Avoid interactions which might lead another teacher to think that you are interested in what they are teaching because they may interpret this to mean that you disapprove of their teaching.' Ultimately, this may all become too complicated so that it is easier to streamline a cluster of informal rules into one. A simplified rule which might incorporate all the meanings of the more complex rules might be: 'Taking about a football match is friendly and safe'. Someone from outside this school might be astounded that such an insignificant rule could be so influential; this rule only makes sense in terms of its aetiology which may not be known.

Although I am not aware of educators who have sought to extensively document the effects of informal rules on schools, such 'fields of rules' have been investigated and articulated in other contexts. Denis Wood and Robert Beck (1994) analyse a family's use of the living room of their house to illustrate this point. In their book, *Home Rules*, they identify 223 specific rules relating to behaviour in the room, safety, and the treatment of the seventy objects it contained. Rule 192, for example, directs members of the household not to press their heads against the aluminium insect screens on the front windows. Rule 222 instructs members not to play with the light switches.

Wood and Beck argue that the rules about how the family members are to treat the physical environment are not only instructive but that they turn a sculpture of various physical materials into a home so that it becomes a cultural creation. Further, the meanings and values that are reflected in the specific rules of that particular room are part of a larger network of rules and customs that are shared by people in their domestic environments across society. The occupants 'live the room' and, in doing so, share a system of beliefs that suggest how people in general live in their domestic environments. The rules are embodied in particular actions and things. The rules create the room as much as the room creates the rules.[2]

Informal rules may be linked together and shape social transactions. Burns and Flam introduce the idea of social grammars by which they mean sets of rules or norms which enable people to structure social transactions differently depending on the status of those present and the setting in which they meet. For example, a school principal and staff present themselves and respond to each other in certain ways because deference to authority is valued in their community. This may be particularly evident at an event such as a school assembly. However, if the head of the state department were the guest of honour, the way in which people present themselves and respond to each other might change. The rules would be transformed. It may be important in this situation for people to dress more formally and behave more deferentially, or, depending on the values attributed to the state department head, it may conversely be more appropriate to represent their deference to authority in terms of a good-natured spirit of cooperation rather than compliance and, in effect, to disguise the actual authority structures.

The interplay of informal rules provides a partial explanation of the durability of school practice. It is conceivable that many of the norms which shape the expectations of teachers in their workplaces are, in fact, fossilized official rules, administrative directives promulgated a long time ago, that have been ritualized and internalized by generations of teachers and have become part of the taken-for-granted landscape. The written rules may have disappeared from the official compendia, or may even be in contravention of current rules and policies, but are part of a professional collective unconscious.

Culture

Events, beliefs, myths, even physical objects, can all be regarded as 'cultural' in that their meaning emerges from shared cultural understandings. Everything we do can be thought of as 'culturally significant' from one point of view or another. At times, it seems that 'culture' is a word conveniently defined by social scientists to explain phenomena that cannot be explained otherwise. Even anthropologists who have their own preferred definitions of 'culture' continue to engage in vigorous debates about the meaning of the word.[3]

What did culture mean to my colleagues who 'blamed' it for the modest achievements of the National Schools Project? Although we used the term often enough we never clarified exactly what we meant by it. In hindsight, I think we considered a 'school culture' to be synonymous with the informal rules or norms of a school staff. These shared beliefs included beliefs about official rules, for example, the belief that it was best to work within the official rules or the belief that they did not have the power to change them. The official rules themselves were things that existed outside the school and therefore were not part of the school's culture. Therefore, use of this definition implied that official rules are not a cultural phenomenon, as far as schools are concerned, but are separate in some way. This assumption, I contend, was mistaken.

Teachers may not know specific details of the Regulations but they do share beliefs about their relevance, their purposes, and the consequences of following or not following the official rules. If they share beliefs that the formal rules are of no consequence but it is their beliefs which are of significance then the formal rules have been dealt a serious blow. They are as good as rescinded. In place of the rules, teaching cultures 'rule' the social context of schooling. It is not surprising that teacher unions, which lack direct power over the formal rules but are well placed to influence teachers' beliefs, choose to put culture on the high altar of school reform.

To define culture exclusively in terms of tacit or locally negotiated rules as distinct from the formal rules has other advantages for teachers. Dichotomizing formal regulation and culture implies that they are distinct entities or opposites. One is concrete and documented; the other obscure and mysterious. Non-teachers inflict the former on teachers; however, teachers assert their power over outsiders who are unable to interpret their informal rules. Culture can mean everything or nothing depending on how the word, or idea, is used. It is mysterious and powerful.

The problem is, however, that the official rules *are* of consequence, and the dominance of culture over regulation is imaginary. It is a false opposition. This fantasy perpetuates the power of the official rules by failing to expose their significance.

There is another way of thinking about culture which encompasses more than just the norms or informal rules which are shared among and distinguish one group of people from another. Culture can be construed as a universe of rules.[4] From this perspective, official rules, as well as informal rules, are a cultural phenomenon. Further, they can be thought of as constituting a cultural 'text', and in doing so, to use Clifford Geertz's famous metaphor, they form 'webs of significance'.[5] The universe of rules is also a system of symbols, a kind of language that is read as though it were a written text. They also form, as Roger Keesing (1987) later wrote, 'webs of mystification as well as signification'. Although many teachers may never have examined, or even seen, the Regulations or the relevant Acts of Parliament, they are well aware of their existence and represent their work as falling within the boundaries that they set. They form part of an overall guidance system within which individuals learn what is expected of them even though they may be unaware of large parts of the system. For example, a deputy principal interviewed by Ray Knight (1996) commented: 'The Regulations are my employer's guidelines for how we should act and conduct ourselves as educators, so to go outside of them is going against what our employer has set down.' She continued: 'And I think we have a loyalty to our employer because they do employ us, so I feel that because [the rules] are set down then we should act within them as far as possible.' (p. 69) Thus, the rules, official and informal, in this general sense 'make the school' just as in my earlier example the rules about how to live in a lounge room make the home. They provide order and consistency and a sense of the importance of a place.

Construing culture in these terms has implications for school reform. Some of the 'universe of rules' constitute school structures. The grouping of students for instructional purposes into class-sized groups is a structural feature of schools. The structure is held in place not only by the beliefs of school staff about optimal arrangements for grouping students but also by regimes of official regulations which require students to be on site during certain hours, cover curriculum content, meet assessment requirements, and so on. The fact that the structures can be subverted by determined teachers does not negate their existence or force. In effect, rules, formal and informal, combine to define and shape structures. Andy Hargreaves puts it this way:

> Cultures do not operate in a vacuum. They are formed within and framed by particular structures. These structures are not neutral. They can be helpful or harmful. They can bring teachers together or keep them apart. They can facilitate opportunities for interaction and learning, or present barriers to such possibilities. (Hargreaves, 1994, p. 256)

It is myopic of present day school reformers to focus on some of the rules constituting structures and ignore others. Bureaucrats are often criticized for placing too great an importance on official rules and ignoring the culture of schools. Ironically, present day 'culturalists' are at risk of erring in the other direction.

At some point, the distinction between official and informal rules becomes arbitrary or irrelevant; active or inactive might be a more helpful way of distinguishing between rules since teachers rarely make practical distinctions between official rules and informal rules. Nevertheless, as discussion often ensues as though informal rules are part of a school's culture and official regulations are not, it is worth exploring and illustrating how the regulations are culturally inscribed.

Official Rules and Teaching Cultures

Official rules can attain a status which is far more significant than that implied by their legal interpretation. To illustrate this, I have selected two examples, one pertaining to the authority of teachers, the other to the authority an education department has over a teacher.

I became aware of the first example when I visited a high school which reputedly had a high turnover of inexperienced staff and a substantial enrolment of difficult students. Pinned on every door I went through was a list of school rules which were similar to lists of rules seen in many schools, although it is probably fair to say that these rules created the impression that the relationships between teachers and students were fairly traditional. At the base of the chart with the rules listed was a reference to the parliamentary Regulations with a section of it quoted: '. . . a teacher has authority to secure the good behaviour of his pupils . . .' (Regulation 28.(2) Education Act Regulations, Education Department of Western Australia, 1960).

I noticed these posters because generally there is no reference or authority cited for such school rules. The question of their legitimacy is normally negotiated among the people in the school who are seen to be the appropriate group for determining such matters. However, in this school it was as though the staff wanted to communicate to all students, and possibly some parents, that a teacher's authority derives from 'the law of the land', a higher authority than that which can be derived from local negotiations. Possibly because of the teachers' lack of experience, their lack of commitment to that community and the short periods of time they spent in the location, they needed to draw on a higher authority than that implied by the purpose of the school and the responsibilities they exercised as educators.

My second example relates to Regulation 86A (Education Act Regulations, Education Department of Western Australia, 1960) which enables the Education Department to impose sanctions against an 'inefficient' 'teacher'. I use parentheses because inefficient and teacher are the actual words used although 'teacher' in this context means any member of staff employed under the Education Act. Given the warp which exists between what is intended by a rule and what it is interpreted to mean, it is likely that the use of the word 'teacher' provided principals and school psychologists with a degree of protection even though it was intended to apply to them also. Regulation 86A is rarely used but it is capable of immobilizing teachers by striking fear in their breasts.

Although Regulation 86A enables the Director General to reduce the status of a 'teacher' who is 'inefficient', the general sentiment among senior officials is that it is very difficult to get this Regulation to 'stick' should it be tested in an industrial court. In the rare instances that it is applied, it is almost always tested in this way. However, as in the case of other regulations, this one has power that exceeds its capacity to be applied in law. It is like a *ju-ju*; its magic means that evil intent is all that is required to destroy those at whom it is directed.

How does the magic work? Here is an example reported to me. A principal of a school where discontented parents had been very vocal was called into the office of the superintendent late in the school year. This was not their first discussion about the principal's difficulties about which he had been open. However, at this point the superintendent informed him that he did not want him to return to the school the following year and that if he insisted on exercising his right to do so then he would invoke proceedings under Regulation 86A.

The principal's assessment of his situation at this point was that he had no choice other than doing as the superintendent wished, namely, to accept a less senior position at another school. He called this 'voluntary retrogression'. The principal was aware of this 'option' and had been considering it anyway, however, once the superintendent stated his intention to commence proceedings under Regulation 86A, the principal believed that he had no option. It was like an incantation. There was no need for the superordinate officer to go through a long and tedious process before making formal recommendations which could then be overturned in an industrial court; the Regulation's power resided in the fear it invoked. This fear may have roots in teaching cultures; it also has roots in official rules of the ilk of Regulation 86A.

The Bensenville New American School Project provides another illustration of how official rules and teaching cultures interact. As already outlined in Chapter 4, the Bensenville project group sought to establish an innovative school which challenged traditional notions of the school as an institution but gave up this dream after planning for it was well under way. Jeffrey Mirel's account of Bensenville suggests that the shared beliefs in the community and the official rules conjoined so that the one supported the other. Neither supported reform. The massive exemptions that would have been required to enable the Bensenville Project to go ahead might unravel the regulatory fabric with which teachers and community members were familiar and comfortable. Such exemptions were seen as unacceptable conditions for the establishment of a new form of schooling.

In this case, the belief that the official rules had to be preserved meant that the ambitious reform initiative which commenced in a climate of optimism came to a stop. The Bensenville community's confidence in the formal regulations acted to perpetuate them; their belief that the regulations existed in order to protect the interests of teachers and the community meant that they could not be challenged. Bensenville illustrates the inseparability of culture and regulation rather than the domination of one by the other.

Yet another example of how formal rules interact with cultures can be drawn from a study of policemen enforcing the law. Egan Bittner argues that police officers on patrol are faced with practical problems which arise because they are trying to keep the peace.[6] Police officers walk along their beats with expectations and knowledge of social norms which enable them to make sense of the activities going on around them. They can recognize and differentiate between normal and unusual events. They also have knowledge of police department directives about what they should do and not do in various circumstances. One of the 'resources' which they can draw on when confronted with a practical problem when on patrol is to invoke 'the law'. In this sense, the officers on duty 'do not really enforce the law when they invoke it, but merely use it as a resource to solve certain practical problems in keeping the peace' (Bittner, 1967, p. 710).

Education rule regimes are used in similar ways. Teachers, principals and bureaucrats decide whether a situation might be improved by applying a rule. If they believe that a rule will help, an attempt will be made to find an appropriate one. If they can see no advantage resulting from the application of a rule, even though there may be clear evidence of an infraction, they will find some reason to ignore the situation. These judgments will be based on much more than just a knowledge of the official rules. They will need to have a sense of what would generally be considered to be a worsening or improvement of the situation and what kind of consequences might be expected if a rule is either applied or not applied. In most cases, officials will not attempt to invoke formal rules unless such an action would be supported by informal rules about fairness. Once again, this illustrates the enmeshment which can be observed between official rules and teaching cultures.

Rules, Culture and the National Schools Project

Although the perception that regulation was restricting school improvement led to the establishment of the National Schools Project, regulation is no longer seen as the central issue among the members of its off-shoot the National Schools Network. Obstructions to reform are now seen in terms of 'culture' not regulation. As Julie Harradine (1996) summarizing research literature on school reform in the Network's newsletter writes: 'most current research holds that the culture of the school is the single most important factor determining the extent to which educational change occurs'. Attitudes such as this have led to the introduction of the term 're-culturation' as the linchpin of school reform.

It is important to understand how this change in emphasis has taken place in order to see what the consequences of it might be. The National Schools Project is typical of reforms referred to as 'waiver projects'. It was founded on the belief that if regulations which constrained teachers' work could be identified and removed, then teachers would be free to adopt pedagogical approaches that were presently restricted and so be more effective. It recognized the importance of the grass roots, relying heavily on teachers to identify the regulations which they considered to be the obstacles.

I surveyed the National Schools Project schools after the Project itself had been concluded. Several of those participants who responded pinpointed culture as the reason why they and their colleagues had not sought a regulatory exemption. For example, a high school project coordinator wrote that a major impediment to change in his school was 'the natural conservativeness of [teaching] staff. . . .There was no real desire to "think outside the square", . . . The idea of paradigm shifts was threatening to conservative staff members . . . Teachers felt constrained by the rules and regulations of the system, but this appeared to be a rationalisation for their own inhibitions and no real attempt was made to challenge the system.' According to this view, not only are the regulations irrelevant but teachers use them unreasonably as an excuse for continuing to apply traditional pedagogies.

In another example, a primary school principal explained the failure of an attempt to challenge primary school pedagogy by engaging high school teachers to work with students. The major impediment from his perspective was the view of the primary school teachers that 'the pedagogy of high school teachers is too content driven and that, as a rule, high school teachers are insufficiently concerned with the needs of the whole child'. This was a sufficient obstacle in itself and so there was no test of whether regulation would impede the implementation of this idea. Interestingly, the principal reported that there were no regulatory impediments despite the fact that the idea had not been presented outside the school.

The departmental and union officials I interviewed also attributed the modest scale of restructuring that occurred during the life of the National Schools Project to the culture of schools rather than official regulations. A director in one state department commented: 'The major impediment, I think, is a cultural thing. In some ways we're still teaching students in a similar fashion to what we have been teaching for many years. . . .Do students have to come to school every day? Can we teach Years 11 and 12 in much larger classes? Should we be looking at different types of teaching or tutorial-type scenarios? I mean, it always reminds me of when I left school and went to university and sat in a very large lecture room where they used to teach Economics 1 and we had over a thousand students in the lecture room.' These questions although obvious ones were never raised by the representatives of the employers during the life of the National Schools Project. To have placed these possibilities on the table in a serious way would have jeopardized the willingness of the union representatives to continue meeting. This director's unwillingness to make such a suggestion was in response to an informal rule or norm which had come to be understood among the participants of the Project: don't suggest anything which the unions will perceive to challenge the formal rules they rely on to uphold teachers' working conditions.

The official attributing the lack of change to 'a cultural thing' among teachers was in fact applying an informal rule which ensures that the teachers' industrial award cannot be challenged. Within the context of a waiver project such as the National Schools Project, to imply that the teachers' industrial award might have a capacity to interfere with change, was to challenge its status and the position of the union. It was not the binary opposition of 'a cultural thing' versus regulatory factors which impeded changes to work organization rules; the culture of what could best be described as 'industrial relations' was operating in a way which protected the formal rules.

By ignoring the complex interactions between the formal and informal rules it was possible to invoke classic works on teaching, such as Seymour Sarason's (1982) *The Culture of the School and the Problem of Change* which attributes the failure of school reform to a lack of understanding of the power and complexity of school culture. The educational research literature on 'effective schools' could also be cited as supporting the significance of school cultures.[7] Officials involved in the National Schools Project were satisfied with this explanation. There were considerable incentives for adopting this position.

On the union side, teachers' salaries and awards achieved through many years of bargaining and industrial action, escaped without a serious challenge. On the employer side, the implication was that the labyrinthine corpus of rules over which government officials presided need not be scrutinized in earnest. The reasons for initiating the Project in the first place had evaporated. There was no need to change any of the things that might make a difference; in fact, union and government officials alike could pat themselves on the back; they had no need to change, it was teachers who needed to change. The factors over which senior officers have influence were found to be not significant after all.

Conclusion

In this chapter, I have argued that in relation to school reform the tendency to attribute considerable influence to school cultures and play down the influence of official rules should be seen as a cultural phenomenon in its own right. I am not arguing that the construct of school culture is necessarily flawed or unhelpful. I accept that school cultures are a major factor influencing teachers' work. However, I question the validity of differentiating between school cultures and the official regulatory framework as though they are distinctly separate constructs, one in opposition to the other. The official rules, in combination with social norms, beliefs, and expectations create the social reality of the school and provide the means by which teachers and officials locate themselves within it.

Waiver projects were established because regulations were seen to be restricting school improvement. Changing practice would be relatively straightforward if all that were involved were the rescinding of a particular rule as sought by the proponents of such projects. Usually, however, a change of practice requires the disintegration of a set of rules that have been bonded together. This is not so straightforward, especially if some of the rules are tacit and deeply embedded in the construction of what staff believe is the 'most appropriate way of doing things'.

Further, the constraint on change may arise not from the force of a particular rule, or even a set of rules, but from the body of rules as a whole. The change of practice may require a different reading of the rules insofar as the rules contribute a cultural text that frames the relationships among the employer and employees, principal and teachers, union leader and members, minister and department head, and by doing so, creates a web of expectancies that transcend the official rhetoric of educational reform. It takes more than rescinding a regulation with a few strokes of a pen or the promulgation of a memorandum to change these power relationships which are embodied in regulations. It is not just culture at work here — it is culture *and* regulation.

Notes

1 Social norms have been the subject of considerable discussion in social psychology for a large part of this century. Sherif (1965) uses the term to describe the common standards or ideas which guide the responses of members in all social groups. Social norms, when they are internalized, induce conformity in the actions of group members and increase group unity. Newcomers have to master the norms to fit into the group.

2 Clifford Geertz (1983) makes a similar point, observing that 'legal thought is constructive of social realities rather than merely reflective of them'. It is helpful, he argues, to go beyond the functionalist view of the law as a device which serves particular purposes, such as defending the rights of the weak, and so on, and to think of it as a means of self-understanding and understanding of others.

3   Thompson (1990) provides a helpful review of different meanings attributed to 'culture' in the academic world. See also Roseberry, 1989.

4   Geertz also defines culture as a 'set of control mechanisms — plans, recipes, rules, instructions (what computer engineers call 'programs' — for the governing of behaviour)'. *The Interpretation of Cultures*, p. 44.

5   Clifford Geertz, *The Interpretation of Cultures*, p. 5. Culture is regarded by symbolic and structural anthropologists as a sign system which can be 'read' as though it were a text. See, as an example of this kind of analysis Boon (1986), for whom 'a culture is always interpreted, never simply experienced, both by those "living" it and by observers "reading" it.' p. 240.

6   As well as guiding action, rules may be drawn upon during the action to make sense of it and after the action has been completed to justify and explain it. The meaning of a situation if not settled once and for all by some literal application of pre-existing rules. Actors continually discover the scope and applicability of rules during the occasions in which they use them. For an elaboration of this argument see Wieder, 1970. Mehan and Wood, 1975 write that all symbolic forms (rules, utterances, gestures) carry a fringe of incompleteness that must be filled in, and filled in differently, every time they occur. The idea of a 'zone' or 'fringe' around each rule within which there is scope for actors to make their own sense of the meaning of the rule provides another way of explaining why participants in a reform program can appear to implement it faithfully yet produce an unexpected outcome.

7   Although one of the tenets of the educational reform literature is that successful reform will most likely be contingent on changing the culture of the organization, the literature is usually tentative about how to do this. See, for example, Davis, 1989.

7   Power and Rules

Power is the central mechanism of regulation in organisations. (Daudi, 1986)

Introduction

To understand how regulation works it is necessary to examine how power is exercised. This is because rules are one of the instruments of power. The converse is also true. To understand how power works it is necessary to understand how it combines with regulation. In this chapter, I examine the balance of power between teachers and officials and how regulations and informal rules are used to maintain this balance of power.

Much of the contemporary school reform literature represents relations between teachers and education officials as an imbalance; the emphasis is placed on the power of officials and the powerlessness of teachers. The imbalance, however, may not be as real or decisive as many might think. Given that the formal rules give officials legal powers, why is it that they are unable to exercise them and *make* reforms work? One plausible reason is that the powers that they exercise are insufficient, or to put it another way, those opposing the reform, principally teachers, also exercise power which they use to nullify the reform. To extend this question, if teachers have the power to resist top–down reform why are they unable to implement and sustain their own reforms? I posit that the reason for this is the greater legitimacy which the formal rules afford to officials exercising power that enables them to block teachers' efforts to act as reformers in their own right.

Of the many definitions and different constructions of power (see Lukes, 1974; Bachrach and Baratz, 1970), I find Foucault's particularly helpful with respect to the argument I am advancing.[1] He puts it this way:

> [Power] is a total structure of actions brought to bear on possible actions; it includes, it induces, it seduces, it makes easier or more difficult; in the extreme it constrains or forbids absolutely . . . the exercise of power consists in guiding the possibility of conduct and putting in order the possible outcome. Basically, power is less a confrontation between two adversaries or the linking of one to the other than a question of government. (Foucault, 1984, p. 427)

By construing power as 'guiding the possibility of conduct' and 'a question of government' rather than an entity or a personal attribute it becomes possible to conceive of it in terms of regulation and self-regulation. Power is not something that is dormant until activated by a new reform though accounts of reform sometimes represent it as so. It is there, incipient in the governance of the school system. Ministers fight in cabinet to retain control of their portfolio and for their budget share. Departmental executives resist the pressure of central government agencies to pull them into line. Unions struggle to preserve the ground they have won from previous industrial battles. Principals seek to elude the control of local superintendents. Parents challenge principals. Teachers fight with school administrators. Pupils resist teachers. There is a constant positioning and re-positioning around perceived interests. This web of countervailing power relationships is a fact of organizational life and school reform must be embedded within it.

The Power of Officials

The Power of Departmental Chief Executives

It would be an error to represent the director of a school system (or the cabinet minister or someone somewhere) as all-powerful even though it is common enough for the occupant of that position to be seen as such. The persons in such positions of supposed authority constantly complain about their hands being tied. Being a successful bureaucrat is about 'positioning oneself,' I was told by one department head. Even the most senior executive has to do this: be watchful of encroachment by outside agencies as well as undermining from within the organization.

The capture of departmental control by cabinet ministers and central agencies has considerably tied the hands of senior bureaucrats although a kind of desultory guerilla warfare goes on. One senior departmental official complained how a central agency was formally revoking delegations of power as a way of gaining central control of all departments, not just the education department. This allowed the central agency to reach directly into schools, bypassing the school system's head. A chief executive in another state system complained how new public sector management legislation had undermined his authority. He gave as an example how he now had to conform to public sector-wide regulations on the transfer of staff which severely limited the flexibility to fill positions in far-flung locations. 'It has whittled away the director general's power, I have no room to move', he said. Central departmental officials see themselves as protecting schools from the ravages of the external agencies.

Union leaders, the traditional foes of the directors general fear the capture of the education department by the central agencies. Unions have no basis for cutting deals with them. A teacher union official lamented how the education department which employed its members had lost a lot of its independence.

> I mean not just from politicians, but within the [state] bureaucracy. Quite often now we will try to negotiate with the Department or want something done

and the Department will say quietly: 'Well yes, we agree that something could be done here but we're going to have to go to the public sector management people and work through them . . . unfortunately the public sector management people don't like education.'

The image that senior executives convey is of beleaguered education departments trying to resist the tide of public sector legislation or at least trying to moderate any unintended dysfunctions that it might produce in their school systems. Not surprisingly, a central agency official with whom I spoke saw things differently. The purpose of the cross-sectoral legislation, he explained, was to increase the flexibility of public sector agencies to manage their operations while at the same time holding the departmental heads more accountable for achieving the government's objectives. It is hard to resist the conclusion that the regulatory controls being imposed upon education officials are, in principle, the same as the controls that education officials are imposing on schools.

Although chief executives in state school systems have considerable power within their departments which they derive from statutes, it would be a simplification to claim that the will of such an individual is uniformly and faithfully expressed through the actions of his or her officials. Central and district offices are filled with officials who are constantly having to balance corporate and self interests. School reforms which have been devised without participation or concurrence of middle-level officials, and which are ideologically in opposition to their beliefs, may receive a lukewarm reception from them. Their level of support may not extend beyond minimal compliance. They may passively resist such reform attempts and even go so far as to situate themselves within an anti-reform faction. Further, irrespective of their ideological positions, middle managers often feel they are the meat in the sandwich. Their capacity to get the job done, as they define it, requires the support of teachers and school administrators whom they relate to on a day-to-day basis. In order to continue to enlist such support they must exercise discretion in their interpretation of the rules.

The Discretionary Power of Officials

Rules both enable and limit the exercise of power. Officials are supposed to use the rules to determine what powers they have and how they are to be exercised. At the same time, rules are expected to provide consistency and predictability in the ways power is exercised by minimizing the opportunities available to officials for arbitrary or selfish exercises of power. Discretion is used as a way of providing officials with freedom required to manage the range of issues with which they are presented. Where officials have to invent the rules for themselves they are supposed to do so in accordance with formal, rational principles, that is, it is assumed that a new rule will be logically consistent with higher-order rules. Rights of appeal may be available to protect individuals from idiosyncratic interpretations of rules.

Most officials with whom I have worked in state education departments would claim that their decision making reflected the 'impersonal order' of the classic Weberian model of bureaucracy, applying the rule regimes fairly and thoughtfully. However, on closer inspection, it can be shown that the classical bureaucratic form of administration does not comfortably fit the facts of contemporary education departments, nor can it adequately explain how subordinates, seemingly without protest, allow senior officials to determine how their interests might best be served.

Officials, I concluded from my interviews, are comfortable with rules provided they can decide whether to apply them and how to interpret them. They have considerable scope to do this. Because organizations, such as education departments, have become so large and complex they can only be governed by rule systems that allow considerable managerial discretion. In place of detailed attention to rules, officials are guided by pragmatic, political frameworks for decision making rather than the legal-rational principles that are meant to steer Weber's ideal system.[2]

Policy is a more flexible instrument of governance than the official rules and is used more often by officials to legitimate their actions. Policy describes intent and is focused on the future. Policies, except in the broadest sense, can be set by officials without reference to state legislatures. Official rules define how things are to be done rather than what is to be done. The rules are seen as more timeless and are expected to apply irrespective of the goals of the organization. Although policies are supposed to be congruent with the official rules, unless the policy is controversial, there may be no check on its congruence. It requires an expert legal opinion and a very full knowledge of the rules to decide whether some intended action is *ultra vires*. In my experience, senior officials are inclined to devise new policies and hope for the best. Two department heads confided to me (though I was hardly surprised) that various policy initiatives were, in effect, illegal. Changes to practice were communicated via memoranda and policy statements. Legislation and subsidiary legislation had not caught up with practice, so to speak.

What about the other rules that ought limit the discretion of officials to issue their own directives? As I have shown in Chapter 2, there is no shortage of rules. However, because they are not well known and many have an ambiguous status the body of official rules does not serve as a check on the powers of the officials except when they are dealing with exceptionally well-informed employees, usually briefed by union legal officers in the course of a dispute. In practice, the official rules are seldom cited during the formal and informal transactions between employees and officials. For an employee to even refer to the rules would be perceived by an official as a challenge to the 'friendly' superordinate–subordinate relationship that officials prefer to maintain. It is more likely that the conversation between teacher and official would centre on policy and if there were some contestation between the two it would be over compliance with policy rather than regulation. The 'problem' would be represented as one of 'lack of understanding' rather than 'defiance'.

Latent Power

Privately, Australian education department and union leaders disapprove of dependency on rules. The caricature of the principal who consults the rule book before every move is a figure of sarcasm. 'These are the people who have the holy writ, these are the Druids with the book', commented a union leader. 'They know if you are going to take a school camp you have got to have all these forms filled out. And it has to be done so far in advance.'

I asked a union official whether teachers were different from other occupational groups. He answered in the affirmative, arguing that the culture of school systems nurtured the dependency of teachers on others to tell them what to do:

> My experience of both areas [blue and white collar unions] is that in a blue collar situation the job delegates in a factory will generally run disputes and negotiations and arguments and represent members themselves, even as far as going to the industrial court and only call in an organiser when they really get out of their depth. Whereas teachers, who have all the literacy and organisational skills and resources at their disposal, reach for the phone and ring up organisers and get them to come to the school when there's the smallest problem. It is, I think, a very dependent sort of culture in which people look to the centre a lot.

Teachers may accept the adjudication of officials without any need to refer to the rules. Their acceptance of a direction may spring from a sense that it is the right thing to do rather than fear of some negative sanction. The internalization of such a subordinate status is a consequence of power. Power of this kind could be used either to introduce change with or without changing the rules, or to maintain the status quo while allowing the rules to change.

Power exercised in this way promotes a kind of self-monitoring and self-adjustment. There is an extensive literature (and debate) in sociology and political science describing how this can happen. To illustrate how the official rules contribute to a surrendering of responsibility to others I will draw on the work of Thomas Popkewitz (1991). Popkewitz contends that multiple and 'regionally' organised procedures, rules, and obligations constitute 'texts' which organize and shape how the world is to be seen, acted on, felt and talked about. These texts are fixed in the patterns of schooling and teacher education, the work of academics and the rhetoric of reform. There is a blurring of the boundaries between our own thoughts and actions and those that are given to us in the practices that form our collective efforts. Charles Lindblom (1990), in less Foucauldian terms, refers to this process as socialization, 'the process by which members of each generation acquire a language, a world view, and a set of rules of the game that specify both the impermissible and the obligatory'. (p. 70)

The official rules constitute one such text, albeit an important one. Others include memoranda, newspapers, newsletters, even ceremonies and performances insofar as the notion of text is broadened. The texts help individuals locate themselves in hierarchies with ascribed rules and obligations relating to their rank: teacher and principal, principal and local superintendent, local superintendent and state department head. The texts also contain a system of rules that govern what talk about education is possible and who should be listened to. Third, the texts contain the 'authorized' interpretation of practice by virtue of what they contain and what they omit. Finally, the texts become a repository of common sense about teaching and schooling. (Popkewitz, 1991, pp. 201–2.)

What constitutes the authorized interpretation? The texts, Popkewitz argues, reflect an instrumental logic where values, interests and choices are made to seem technical matters. Standardized and routinized procedures are emphasized, while the relationships among the various elements and their relationship to the whole are exempt from scrutiny. They can be incorporated in the existing decision-making structures without need for open debate or a renewed mandate. There is no need for coercion or to invoke the official rules. The rational 'discourse' of reform should be viewed as a form of regulation, self-regulation and monitoring which governs the system so that the very possibility of thinking 'outside the square' (as one of the teachers I cited earlier commented) is substantially reduced.

But the foregoing analysis leaves me with a problem: if there is a dominant discourse and if it has such a rationalist, instrumental strain, why is it that school reforms, formulated in these terms and driven with the authority of the government and the teachers' employer, fail to succeed in taking root in schools?

Consider the power of officials. They have specific legal powers derived from statutes allowing them even to dismiss employees. They have discretionary powers to interpret regulations in ways that favour or hinder the fortunes of employees. They occupy positions in an organizational hierarchy with all the accoutrements of office that signal that they should be treated with the deference traditionally shown to the occupants of senior positions. How can teachers but comply?

The Power of Teachers

The Limits of the Power of Officials

The arm of even the most senior bureaucrat is not long enough to reach into every classroom. Power has to be delegated. The street-level bureaucrats, who then use the rules, may see things differently from their chief executive. In any event, department heads fight wars on other fronts that seem remote from the concerns of teachers. The rules that legitimize coercion are there but are seldom invoked: officials have to occupy the high moral ground before doing so and unions make that difficult to achieve. Management prerogative can only be used so often. Eventually, implementing policy becomes a matter of 'doing business'. For officials responsible for invigilating the rules and putting policy into effect rules can take on a different meaning when observed from the position of teachers on the lower deck. The situation never quite fits the rules.

Teacher unions, of course, when they are able to represent the views of teachers, have power that reaches into schools. The special set of rules derived from industrial relations legislation that apply to employers and unions equally, if invoked, place teachers and officials on a more even footing. Changes to work organization that would disturb the 'regularities of schooling' fall under the jurisdiction of courts that have the power to direct education departments to stop reform. The courts also have promulgated rule regimes which spell out how disputes are to be resolved. These powers have been put in place to prevent employers overriding the rights of workers. Where unions can represent their opposition to reform as legally sanctioned, or where unions can cast doubt on the legality of the employers' reforms, they provide their members in schools with an official basis of resisting reform.

A Case Study of Power Relations

I will illustrate the limits of the power of officials by describing the experiences of a teacher, Rodney Grant, who while acting in the role of union convener in his school, sought to clarify the extent and limits of his principal's authority to direct staff.[3] The events occurred during a prolonged and bitter industrial dispute. The issues that were contested were complex and changed during the course of the dispute. One issue was the fairness of new industrial relations laws which had the potential to curtail the role of unions in setting salaries and conditions of work. Another was the package of trade-offs demanded in return for a salary increases: the trade-offs included fixed amounts of professional development in teachers' own time and, a sacred cow — local selection of staff. When the union felt it was unlikely to make any further progress it banned voluntary work by its members in order to demonstrate to the government and the public at large the contribution that teachers made in their own time.

During the dispute, which ran for over a year, the principal and staff members at Grant's school were placed under tremendous pressure. The principal was expected to serve as a functionary in the line management structure. In strongly unionized schools, when the principal accepted this role, principal and teachers were set against each other. The nature of these conflicts is illustrated by a conversation between Grant and his school's principal, which he recounted. At the time, the particular problem that the principal was trying to solve was how to re-activate curriculum meetings which were an essential part of the school management process but had previously been banned by the union branch as part of a general directive against undertaking work out of school hours.

> The principal said he would instruct us [the teaching staff] to attend meetings which were subject to industrial bans so I said to him, 'How are you going to do that?'

He said, 'What if I call a meeting of all the staff and say, "Move to your curriculum areas within the staff room and conduct your subject meetings"'.

I said to him, 'What happens if no-one moves?' He said to me, 'What do you mean?' and I said, 'What happens if we all passively resist?'

Grant was acting in his role as union convenor. The situation was delicately balanced and highly charged. In this instance the principal kept his powder dry. Reflecting on this exchange Grant observed:

No one knows how much authority the principal really has. It's extraordinary but no-one really knows. I suppose my view was that he couldn't make us do something we didn't want to do although it isn't really clear whether this is the case or not. You can refer to the Regulations but they don't actually tell you, so if you don't test it then you will never find out.

At times, Grant sought advice from the union's central office which gave direction on some matters, however, there were times when its staff members were unable to clarify the extent of a principal's authority. On one occasion the dispute came to a head.

I remember a teacher who was really upset. He was a strong bloke and determined to keep to the union's line. As a result of receiving an Education Department directive, the principal told him to do something which was subject to industrial bans and that, if he didn't do it, he and his staff would have pay docked until they complied with the Education Department directive.

In the super-heated industrial climate, the threat was taken seriously. Some teachers were fearful of losing their jobs. Grant sought advice from the union.

Interestingly, the union's advice regarding that instance was for the teacher to do as the principal had instructed him because the union wasn't sure where it stood and it's funds were low because of the industrial action. So the thinking was that it was risky to rely on the question being answered in court. So we took their advice on that one.

The events in Grant's school were repeated in hundreds of others. By passively resisting, the union members increased the public pressure on the government. At one point during the dispute the government decided to produce a new regulation, Regulation 25, which would strengthen its mandate to compel teachers to participate in educational activities out of hours. An industrial court advised that a draft regulation was *ultra vires*, that is, it was incompatible with the objects of the existing industrial relations legislation.

The incident illustrates the ambiguity that existed about the authority of the principal. It also illustrates the insufficiency of the power of official regulation to produce reform. With the whole weight of the existing Regulations behind it, Education Department officials were unable to compel teachers to follow what many members of the public might regard as reasonable directions. Clutching at straws, they wanted one more regulation. Where authority seemed clear-cut at the outset, it seemed less so when the complexities were revealed and unravelled. Formal regulations were *used* in the dispute but were not sufficient to resolve it.

Power in the National Schools Project

The language of the Australian National Schools Project was always couched in terms of empowering teachers professionally and linking this to productivity. The culture was not one in which naked use of power was acceptable; it was a new culture created to develop a shared understanding which could provide a context within which the different interests could coax each other into consensual deals.

It was agreed early in the Project's life that it would not adopt a reform-by-edict approach. The senior participants had had sufficient experience to recognize the problems associated with this. Rather, the improvements would result from the work of teachers in pilot schools who would make recommendations through the steering committees in each state.

The bottom-up ethic of the Project was to operate within definite constraints. After all, the Project was essentially a coalition of opposing power blocks each of which was rooted in the traditions of adversarial industrial relations. Proposals were only welcome from a small number of schools which had been persuaded that there were benefits tied to participation. The staff in these schools then attended courses run by Project officers and had to demonstrate that their proposals reflected the views of the majority of school community members before they could expect them to be considered by a state steering committee. Teachers in pilot schools had no representation on these state-level committees. Although it was never intended that classroom teachers be junior partners, it would not be surprising if some of them felt this way at times. Certainly, there were no challenges to the authority of state committees.

The staff in these schools were in the invidious position of having to deal not only with the senior departmental and union representatives involved in the Project but also with their local departmental and union officials who had day-to-day contact on operational matters. Many may have made a realistic assessment that the Project could not protect those who challenged the authority of either the union or department after its three years had expired. Cost-benefit calculations would reasonably be made about what might be achieved within the opportunities and constraints provided by the Project.

The National Schools Project was promoted as an unprecedented alliance between unions and employers to improve teaching and learning in schools. Antagonists became partners. On the face of it, the alliance, backed by the Federal government, exercised tremendous power, surely enough to tip the balance in favour of fundamental reform in patterns of work organisation. The pilot schools were all hand picked or volunteers. Here was an ideal re-alignment of power relationships, or so it seemed. Below the surface, however, and outside its Governing Board meetings, the huge majority of officials, from both unions and education departments, owed nothing to the National Project, so went about business as usual. The 'government' of the system, of which the Project was one small, loosely connected part, was left untouched.

Conclusion

Officials are in powerful positions. In some situations, the official rules can become superfluous; relationships between teacher or principal and official may be based on the tacit understanding that it is the responsibility of the former to anticipate what the latter wants and, further, to act on this without necessarily being instructed to do so or without reference to the rules. Employees learn from their more senior colleagues, upon whom rest their prospects for advancement in the organization, that compliance is valued more than independence. Under these circumstances rules may provide a *post hoc* legitimation of actions rather than principally guide them. This is made easier in organizational cultures where the official rules are tangential to decision making and where there is a tendency to look to those in authority to provide solutions to problems.

The rules are part of a wider apparatus that legitimizes the power of officials and symbolizes the rightfulness of their decisions. The existence of most official regulatory frameworks suppresses any initiative to challenge decisions. That this can happen is an important part of the argument of this study because it explains how teachers may feel satisfied with the official rules even though the rules may shape what they do in ways that they would prefer that they did not.

However, officials are not all-powerful. Although employers (and some others, such as teacher union officials and parents) have power over teachers and principals in so far as they can require them to follow the official rules, teachers and principals, on the other hand, can choose to ignore these rules where they are not strictly enforced, or passively resist them where they are. They can actively subvert them through professional networks. In publicly frustrating the achievement of a government's objectives by skilful positioning of the school staff and the community they have power over their employer. Power relations are a two-way street. Thus acceptance of, or resistance to, reform can be construed as compliance with or contestation of rules.

Teachers are happy to rely on the decisions of officials provided that the officials are not seen to be planning to overturn the existing order of the school. They do not mind, or at least can tolerate, changes, small scale changes, that constitute an embroidering of the existing order. Major upheavals, however, activate the power networks.

Thus teachers may successfully resist the attempts of officials to impose flexible grouping patterns in place of groupings based on maximum class-size parameters but on another site or on some other occasion officials may resist attempts by a school to restructure its program around flexible class groupings. In both cases, the union and departmental officials are likely to cite official rules and argue that the reform constitutes a breach of the rules.

The combination of power and regulation constitutes a force much better able to block than enable reform. The net result of the activation of the dominant power relationship is a stalemate, a settlement in two parts which can be put in these colloquial terms: 'You can stop us doing what we want but you can't make us do what you want'. These words could as easily be spoken by teachers referring to officials as officials referring to teachers.

Notes

1 For a review of Foucault's ideas on power and how they fit into the mainstream political science view of power, see Hoy, 1992.
2 Galligan (1990) observes that with the development of the modern state since the latter part of the nineteenth century there has been a growth in state regulation and a concomitant extension of powers delegated to officials to be exercised at their discretion. There has also been an increase in the levels of unauthorized discretion where officials have assumed the power to selectively enforce legal standards. This can be explained partly by the magnitude of the regulatory enterprise which has necessitated delegation, but also by the acceptance of legislatures that many regulatory problems are essentially technical or scientific matters best managed by specialist authorities. (p. 73) Another factor has been the pressure on governments to produce results. In textbooks on public administration the test of good administration is achievement of outcomes and not whether there has been a faithful adherence to fixed rules. Further, the growth in diversity of interests, groups and values in modern societies has exaggerated the complexity of government. Sub-systems within a society develop in order to simplify or reduce the complexity. This has enabled legal regulation to be extended over any area of activity for whatever reasons seem fit, a shift from principles to pragmatism. Legal regulation may then distort reality by imposing formal rules or may consist of extremely abstract statements that provide little practical guidance.
3 This account is based on several interviews with the teacher. I have altered in some minor respects details which might reveal the identity of the teacher and the school.

8   Meta-rules

Rules govern all aspects of experience, what we are to experience, and what not to experience, the operations we must and must not carry out, in order to arrive at a permitted picture of ourselves and others in the world. (Laing, 1976)

Introduction

In this chapter, I explore the question of how rules about rules impact on school reform. I refer to these 'rules about rules' as meta-rules. I begin by outlining the development of this concept in fields other than school education. I then investigate the usefulness of the construct in explaining how people make judgments about which rules or sets of rules they will apply when confronted by the demands created by school reform initiatives. I give an account of a school's attempt to obtain an exemption from a regulation as an illustration of how meta-rules act to maintain the status quo. I also use the construct of meta-rules to explain the results of the Australian National Schools Project.

My argument is that the rules about rules, meta-rules, play a key part in determining whether, when and how both official and informal rules are applied and how authority, power and influence are exercised. An important aspect of meta-rules is that they assist people to determine where they stand in relation to those exercising power. Despite this, meta-rules may be difficult to identify because they are often taken for granted or, possibly even, denied.

Rules about Rules

R.D. Laing discusses how meta-rules operate in the context of the politics of family relationships. Laing, who describes many of the actual rules which operate in families, also describes rules about how these rules apply. He claims that family meta-rules, in dysfunctional families at least, dictate that the rules should remain invisible and that they not be identified or discussed. For example, to articulate a rule about cleanliness may weaken the rule; it is more powerful to assume that all family members are clean and always will be clean from which it follows they have no need of a rule which excludes dirtiness. These silent, shared expectancies which obviate the need for written or spoken rules Laing calls meta-rules.

Burns and Flam (1987), like Laing, argue that meta-rules limit opportunities for reflection, questioning and uncertainty. They describe a basic stability in rule compliance which results:

> . . . because actors adhere to a meta-rule usually acquired and strengthened during child socialization, that social rule systems are 'good', useful, and sooner or later rewarding. And moreover, the costs of opposing them and trying to adopt or create alternative systems are formidable, and most attempts fail. (p. 22)

Burns and Flam also contend that meta-rules enable people to determine what kind of rule system is in effect or how knowledge of meta-rules can be used to transform the rules in operation in a particular situation. They develop the idea that one of the most important differentiations people need to be able to make is between real or serious activity and pretend or play activity. As an example, they use the case of one person kissing another which can create a wide range of significant meanings that most competent adults are able to distinguish adequately. A playful kiss may be considered enjoyable or a breach of acceptable behaviour depending on what sort of rules are in effect. There can be serious consequences for anyone who misjudges such a situation.

Aaron Wildavsky uses a concept similar to that of Laing's concept of meta-rules when explaining how welfare entitlements in the United States are determined in a way which results in higher expenditure. Wildavsky argues that, ironically, the changes which produced higher expenditure can be attributed to a shift in community values about the responsibilities of the government versus the individual; over time the individual came to be seen as less blameless and less deserving of welfare payments. Combined with this shift in public opinion was a heightened concern about equity of welfare provision so that one person's entitlement applied automatically to others in similar circumstances. The result of this drift in community attitudes exacerbated the pressure on the officials, the street-level bureaucrats, whose job it was to determine the eligibility and entitlements of welfare applicants, particularly those officials whose personal values were challenged by the tougher public attitudes to welfare. As a result, they adopted several implicit rules for resolving uncertainty. First, they assumed that it was better to give to the undeserving than to withhold from the deserving. Second, it was thought better to give too much rather than too little. And third, they accepted that the need of welfare recipients justified the cost of welfare benefits. These rules have a moral consistency, according to Wildavsky (1979). He argues that 'a belief that some people's need matters more than some people's money' summarizes the moral meaning that was attached to collections of judgements after they have been made.

> Even if such a rule is not explicitly formulated, it may be implicit in the actions of decision-makers: no law will be passed that values exclusion over inclusion of beneficiaries. Thus, whether or not the rule is specifically stated, one may speak of these laws and regulations on social welfare as if they operated in conformity with such rules. (p. 90)

Despite the absence of the term meta-rule and the different context, Wildavsky and Laing are describing similar phenomena. They both identify abstract rules about how rules are applied which can be deduced from behaviour rather than utterances. In both cases these rules about rules have their origins in moral positions and core values which can permeate social relationships without necessarily being planned or even understood by those holding them.

Though other scholars have made reference to meta-rules, or at least a like-concept (see Mills and Murgatroyd, 1991; Brady, 1987),[1] the references to Burns and Flam, Laing and Wildavsky, writers who incidentally, come from quite different branches of the social sciences, adequately provide a context for my definition of 'meta-rules'. This definition springs from an interview with a senior departmental executive who made a reference to the concept of meta-rules without using the actual term. We were exploring the paradox that the official texts of rules were seldom referred to yet the system functioned as though it were rule governed.

> When I ran things, I never bothered to consult these things [acts and regulations], but I think we all have at the same time a sort of frame of reference that has been absorbed into our background and within which we make decisions.

I agree with his observation that decision-making takes place within 'a sort of frame of reference that has been absorbed into our background' which transcends the rules found in rule books. I contend that this 'frame of reference' is defined by meta-rules. To put it simply, meta-rules constitute the over-arching frame of reference for action. These hidden or unstated rules which serve an executive function over other rules, both official and informal, are rarely identified and debated before they are applied. To acknowledge them suggests choices which many would rather deny, preferring instead to present a particular course of action as inevitable once a situation and its constraints are known. To question the inevitability of such a course of action is often represented as a failure to understand how things really work or in terms of moral inadequacies as meta-rules are often framed in terms of moral concerns.

I argue that meta-rules have an important function in regard to school reform which is not well understood but which requires explanation. The frame of reference within which decisions about school reform take place can be construed as a set of meta-rules which:

1   create expectations which are shared among the members of a group;
2   are used to bridge the inconsistencies which exist among the myriad of individual rules and conflicting rule systems;
3   are concerned with definitions of power relationships;
4   are likely to be tacit and may run counter to stated positions;
5   differentiate between rules which are serious and those which can be ignored; and
6   serve an executive function in regard to other rules.

Meta-rules and Discourse

Before illustrating how meta-rules come into play in educational settings I will consider briefly the concept of 'discourse'. I have already made several references to it. This is because the construct of discourse is a useful way of linking power and meta-rules. Also, it has become a frequently used concept in the social sciences, often associated with the writings of Michel Foucault and Jurgen Habermas among others.

A discourse is a language of an institution. Its members share rules or expectations that govern not only what is said but what kinds of things are (normally) sayable, whether as trivial conversation or polished speech. A discourse defines what kinds of performances are appropriate in particular situations. The knowledge and power that is attached to who can speak and what they can say is unevenly distributed among the positions available to people. Members of organizations occupy roles and each role situates the member in a position of relative power — or powerlessness — and is accompanied with a strong sense of what would be 'natural' speech and behaviour for anyone who occupies it. Thus power is exercised through patterns of exchanges.[2]

Because a discourse determines what may be said, whether what is said can be believed, and who can say it and expect to be believed, an 'unauthorized' speaker may be labelled a troublemaker or a fool. On the other hand, a bland memorandom from a senior official about some apparently trivial matter reminds the reader of their respective positions in the bureaucratic structure. The memo conveys more than the trivial administrative matter.

The commentary on discourse is permeated with references to power and control though there is seldom reference to rules as such, other than those relating to language use. This may be because the notion of rule commonly implies a rational, considered response to a directive whereas discourse implies an unseen, uncomprehended positioning of actors in power relations. Yet the notion of meta-rule as I have elaborated above also implies a taken-for-granted attitude to one's position in a power structure.

Meta-rules are woven into the fabric of discourse. They become rules of discourse. Earlier I discussed at some length the argument of Thomas Popkewitz that the instigators of recent national and state school reform initiatives used a highly rationalist, technicist discourse which exempted them from having to justify to teachers the educational grounds for their interventions in their schools. Another way to represent Popkewitz's formulation would be to describe the meta-rules embedded in the discourse. I will illustrate this using my own example in the chapter that follows.

The arena of reform is complicated by the functioning of multiple discourses. In addition to the discourse of 'the reformers' — the officials acting on behalf of the government — there are also discourses, for example, those associated with teacher unionism and the law. Consider the former, teacher unionism. Through its newspapers, meetings, local branch structures and profile in the media, unionism is a part of the institutional life of schools. During disputes over salary claims which are now inevitably tied to reform, meta-rules of unionism come into play, meta-rules such as, 'Individual benefits must be represented in terms of the greater good'. A tacit quality gives these rules special power. For example, solidarity is an article of faith. There would be no point in challenging the primacy of collective interest over individual interest from within the union movement since to do so would challenge more than a century of tradition. It may even be difficult to question what such a concept as 'the greater good' actually means to members because to do so may imply a disrespect for shared beliefs. Whatever the wording of the official union rules this principle would reign uncontested because to contest such a fundamental meta-rule would lead to self-exclusion. Hence, meta-rules frame the way members interpret their own rules of association as well as the employers' rules of work organization.

Meta-rules and Teaching

Laing's examples of meta-rules are drawn from childhood experiences about socialization. The principles may be applied to school organizations and teaching. Consider the case of some important aspects of teachers' work which are assumed to occur without being specified in employment contracts. An example of this is marking students' work. To introduce a rule requiring teachers to mark students' work in their own time would be considered unacceptable and might actually lead to a reduction of marking during out-of-school hours. This is not because teachers are unwilling to mark students' work but rather because the rule is antagonistic; to introduce it suggests that teachers are not doing their work adequately whereas most teachers do a considerable amount of work in addition to their instructional commitments even though the extent of their commitment is often not acknowledged or understood. Thus, the *absence* of an official rule requiring teachers to mark students' work as an additional duty ensures that marking is completed in 'their own time'; the possibility of this not occurring can hardly be contemplated. This is an example of how teachers can be subject to a moral obligation which may be more difficult to question than matters dealt with explicitly in their employment agreements. Self-regulation can be more powerful than an external mandate.

Catherine Marshall, Douglas Mitchell and Frederick Wirt (1989) describe a set of rules which they call the 'the rules of the game'. These were observed operating among education policy makers seeking to influence decisions. Some of these function in similar ways to the meta-rules described by Burns and Flam although the terms 'behavioural principles' and 'operational principles' are used.

One of the rules of the game which Marshall and her colleagues identify is cited as an example; they called this rule, 'Something for everyone'. This rule is required because it is often necessary to build a political consensus among competing interest groups in order for a bill or policy to be endorsed. Benefits and losses must be shared and seen to be shared among various constituencies. A state superintendent is quoted as explaining the successful passage of new curriculum regulations: 'No one got everything he wanted but [all group representatives] were able to see that no one else got everything they wanted either' (p. 94). The application of an 'operational principle' explained why it was possible to adopt changes. Although the term meta-rule is not used there are aspects of the 'Something for everyone' rule which resemble a meta-rule.

An Example in Context

I will give an example from one of the pilot schools during the National Schools Project. In order to improve teaching and learning, the staff members in this school decided to focus on collaboration in both school decision making and teaching. To make this work they presented a proposal to the Project's state steering committee about the re-allocation of time. The idea was to spend an hour each week meeting after school and to close the school several days early at the end of the year to pay teachers back for the time they had foregone. In the first year, the proposal was accepted by the Projects' state steering committee and passed on to the Minister who formally exempted the school from the relevant regulation.

The change process built up a head of steam in the school but there were divisions in the school between staff who did not mind how many hours they spent attending meetings after school and those who preferred not to participate at all. It was decided that there could be problems if reluctant teachers were required by the majority to participate on a 'voluntary' basis. As a consequence, it became more important to formally reallocate time in the second year than it had been in the first. This proved to be problematic, however, after a state election which resulted in a change of government.

Meanwhile problems were being experienced more generally in the Project. The new Minister for Education was suspicious of the National Schools Project and was philosophically opposed to partnerships with unions. Officials working on the Project were concerned about saving it from complete annihilation. It was thought that the best way of doing this was to avoid drawing the Minister's attention to anything he might disapprove of. Without anyone really knowing for sure, it was thought that the Minister would see the re-allocation of time proposal as a back door attempt by the union to shorten the school year by forty hours which would cast a shadow over the state's continuing participation.

The strategy for dealing with this problem was to establish a regulation which gave the education department head power to exempt schools from regulations. This was supported by the Minister but stopped by a Parliamentary committee on the grounds that as the Minister made the regulations only the Minister could authorise exemptions from them.

A request that the school be exempted from a regulation which would allow it to close early was never presented to the new Minister, however, as one of the teachers in the school reported, 'No-one ever said that we couldn't close the school early.' There was, after all, a precedent from the previous year and the local superintendent was sympathetic. The fact that the school contravened the Education Act Regulations when it closed early did not seem problematic by that stage.

The events surrounding this school's application for an exemption from a regulation provide some insight into the complexities which surround reform efforts in real life. Even when union and departmental officials invite teachers to test out rules, teachers are justified in proceeding with caution. On the surface, an official rule is merely a written mandate that can be deleted by striking a few keys on a word processor. Below the surface, a rule is a manifestation of an approved way of operating that may be passively or actively contested. Further, the rule may be symbolic of a much wider field of action than that which it literally governs.

This school was not stopped from taking initiative even though it may have been had it made any petulant demands or drawn attention to its plight. There were a number of factors which made the changes possible; the superintendent, the principal and the union members in the school were all on the same side, staff members were industrious and trusting and didn't complain when they failed to obtain the formal approval that had been expected and there was the precedent of the early closure having been approved the previous year.

Although some changes were made in one school, the status quo in terms of the regulatory framework within which the school operated was maintained. To some extent the members of this school community were required to 'play the system', 'know their place', ensure that there was 'something for everyone' and 'build on past practice' to ensure that they were not penalized for taking initiative. By accepting these meta-rules which reflected the dominant values about how rules should be applied, they escaped sanctions even though the regulation about schools remaining open until a certain date was breached. This could be represented as a double bind; because they accepted that it was necessary to obtain approval for their actions they were not stopped from proceeding when, through no fault of their own, Ministerial approval was not available. The freedom to test the rules was gratuitous.

Meta-rules within the National Schools Project

Like all reform initiatives, The National Schools Project had its own rules. Its official rules were thrashed out by the participating officials, endorsed by a Governing Board and communicated through memoranda and newsletters. Its *informal* rules were in many regards unique because the diversity of groups with representation meant that participants originated from very different systems. These differences included: Commonwealth and state governments, unions and employers, and, public and private education systems. The differences had to be respected as did the 'bottom lines' of groups with substantial influence.

The National Schools Project functioned as a delicate political alliance. Remarkably, there were no resignations during the three years that the Project continued. Most of the informal rules that developed were designed to keep the parties around the table; the matters which could split the group were well understood. There was an implicit rule that a matter which would fracture negotiations could not be tabled; to raise a matter of difference was to risk representing oneself as someone who didn't understand how things work. The price paid for 'understanding' was compromise and ambiguity; it was better to forego a claim or to leave it unresolved than to split the alliance.

In order to understand how the Project worked in practice and why it ultimately achieved little of what it set out to achieve, it is necessary to describe some of the compromises that were made along the way. First, the conventional rules of research were ignored. The selection of pilot schools varied from state to state but, in general, they were screened to ensure that no strongholds of anti-union or anti-employer sentiment were included.[3] They were neither a random selection nor a group of schools selected for their interest or track record in reform. If anything, they were a group of schools where teachers were likely to be aware of the delicate balance in union and employer claims upon them.

Second, the pilot schools were under pressure to follow a particular line in relation to the offer of regulatory exemption. The early rhetoric was persuasive but as it turned out, the teachers' union position contained a number of bottom lines. These were never formally declared or debated among the members of the Governing Board. Although it was unstated, it became clear that the unions would not consider any weakening of award conditions or anything that might be perceived as such. They also excluded the possibility of solutions which involved any form of trade-off involving less paid teacher time or increased workloads for teachers. They were strongly opposed to the 'casualization' of staffing as they put it — the replacement of full-time positions with multiple part-time positions — in such cases union memberships were at stake. These bottom lines were only referred to obliquely or dismissed as though no-one could have seriously expected to support an obvious threat to award conditions. The employer representatives turned a blind eye to this interpretation of the Project rules as long as they held out hope that some of the pilot schools would propose radical variations of student groupings which would introduce different mixes of teachers and ancillary staff and more flexible hours of instruction. When it became evident during 1993 that the Project would not provide the ammunition for an assault on the work organization conventions, the Project had lost its original direction.

A third compromise was an acceptance that the unions could expect their members in the pilot schools to uphold their core values. There was little challenge to this because the employers' saw no benefits in collaboration or networks and put less time and thought into the Project over all. The unions, on the other hand, recognized the benefits of working together and supporting their members in the pilot schools and reaped rewards as a result.

It would be unfair to represent the union and departmental officials as exercising overt power over pilot schools as there was no evidence that this occurred. However, controls were in place. Never, during the three year course of the Project did a participant apply pressure to the steering committee to challenge its authority to make the ultimate decisions or even to reverse a decision.

Although the rhetoric of the Project extolled the virtues of challenging rules and impediments to flexibility, a powerful rule, I argue this was a meta-rule, influenced the many detailed decisions which were made under the umbrella of the Project. The meta-rule was: 'No one can be expected to agree to anything which will extend someone else's power or limit their own'. This was never stated or debated, however, it could be deduced by any participant either in one of the Project's state steering committees or the pilot schools. This message was embedded in the relationships which were played out in the life of the Project; it was part of the discourse.

The meta-rule about the preservation of power was never put on the agenda. To have done so would have been to challenge the bona fides of the participants. However, by accepting that this meta-rule had precedence over other rules, deep divisions between participants could be camouflaged by camaraderie and the Project could continue against the odds. Unfortunately, however, it also meant it could not achieve the goals it began with.

Conclusion

Meta-rules are rarely identified and discussed before being applied. Many people making use of them would prefer not to acknowledge that they have choices about which rules they will apply in any given situation. Rather, they prefer to take action in a manner which assumes that a particular course is inevitable given a situation and its constraints. To question the inevitability of such a course of action is to imply a failure to understand how things really work or, even, the importance of moral issues, as meta-rules are often framed in these terms.

In the next chapter, I develop the concept of meta-rules further by providing an account of a school principal's efforts to break the mould provided by a public school system.

Notes

1   Brady, 1987 uses the term meta-rule but gives it a more limited meaning. He defines meta-rules as rules that enable actors to make exceptions to rules. Brady identifies two such meta-rules which administrators can give as rationalizations for applying or making exceptions to rules. The first of these he calls the 'principle of benefaction' which enables an exception to be made when greater overall good will occur

as a result. He calls his second meta-rule the 'principle of membership' because it enables greater inclusiveness. Although it might be argued that Brady's meta-rules are a form of rules about how rules should be applied, they are presented within a rational framework without reference to the ambiguities and conflicts which exist in formal rule systems. Therefore, he does not propose that they have an executive function which assists individuals to make choices among different sets of rules. Rather, Brady implies that decisions can be categorized according to which of his meta-rules they best support. In this sense, he is more interested in classifying rules than in understanding the judgments people make when they apply them.

2   According to Foucault (1979) discourse is the governing and ordering medium of every institution. Foucault writes:

> Silence itself — the things one declines to say, or is forbidden to name, the discretion that is required between different speakers — is less the absolute limit of discourse, the other side of which is separated by a strict boundary, than an element that functions alongside the things said, with them and in relation to them within overall strategies. There is no binary division to be made between what one says and what one does not say; we must try to determine the different ways of not saying such things, how those who can and those who cannot speak of them are distributed, which type of discourse is authorised, or which form of discretion is required in either case. There is not one but many silences, and they are an integral part of the strategies that underlie and permeate discourses. (p. 27)

3   Some states, such as New South Wales, called for nominations and then state union and employer officials selected the pilot schools from the pool. In other states, such as Western Australia, the pilot schools were hand picked.

9   Meta-rules in Action

> Obey your leaders and submit to them; for they are keeping watch over your souls, as men who will have to give account. Let them do this joyfully, and not sadly, for that would be of no advantage to you. (Paul, 'Letters to the Hebrews', 17)

Introduction

In this chapter, using a case study of a suburban high school, I will illustrate how meta-rules maintain stasis. The school, Willetton Senior High School, sought exemptions from the official rules, gained some but not all that it wanted, tested the limits, broke several meta-rules and finally was steered back into the mainstream.

Meta-rules are not usually listed anywhere. Often their existence has to be inferred. I explained in Chapter 8 why this is so. They are easier to glimpse, however, when they are broken and the offender is brought into line, although, even in these circumstances, the sanction may ostensibly be for breaking an official rule rather than the meta-rule. The resultant wave of gossip and the apocryphal stories shared among colleagues that follow the imposition of sanctions gives the meta-rules new life and restores, or enhances, their salience. In this way the stories, and the implied meta-rules contained in them, contribute to the mythology of the school system. The stories about Willetton are now used to communicate meta-rules, the most general of which is: 'Don't position yourself too far in front of the pack'. Several people told me that this, or words to this effect, was the main message they had understood from the Willetton story.

I accept that there is no single 'true' story of the events that unfolded at Willetton over a period of seven or eight years. As in Kurosawa's film *Rashomon*, the construction depends upon what part, if any, the author played in the events. I will declare my own bias and accept that from the point of view of a staunch unionist, a central office manager, or a school administrator sidelined as a result of the internal restructuring, the story might be a different one.

The Reforms at Willetton

Pushing the Limits

The school came to my attention during 1988. I was then a senior executive responsible for the implementation of the system-wide reforms intended to make schools more self-managing. A colleague asked me, had I heard the latest news about Willetton? Brendon Davies, the school's principal, had convened an annual general meeting to discuss the future of the school which 2000 parents and members of the community had attended. They had packed the school's hall and had overflowed into the foyer and surrounds. This news was hard to believe since in my experience it was difficult to get double-digit numbers of parents to school meetings. From my point of view, Willetton was obviously a school to keep an eye on. In fact, since its foundation in 1977, the school had acquired a reputation as an experimental, 'flexible area' secondary school, established at the tail end of the period in which open plan school designs were being introduced. Davies, however, was setting a new course for the school.

During Davies' first year as principal the school participated with six others in a waiver project.[1] The seven schools in this project had been encouraged to experiment with structural changes to work organization. At the end of the year, the union representative on the project steering group wrote that a perception had developed that

> . . . the schools in the project have the right to 'break rules'. This is a major oversimplification of the project's intentions. This has had the effect of raising alarm for a wide variety of people. Although the final outcome of the project may be reviewing some regulations and conditions of work, it would appear that some participants were unclear about the process, negotiations and the time required for this to occur. (Ministry of Education, n.d., p. 11)

The union withdrew its support for the project the following year as relations with the Education Department broke down. During its involvement in the project, Willetton generated a number of proposals that tested the union and Education Department: paying teachers to cover classes of absent colleagues and authorizing staff to leave the school premises when not scheduled for teaching are two examples. Also, during this period the school reviewed its decision-making procedures, the result of which was agreement to establish a school board composed of equal numbers of school staff and community members as well as a staff executive composed of members elected from among the staff and administrators occupying newly created positions, including Director of Operations, Director of Curriculum and Director of Student Services. On the educational front, the school signalled its intention to develop its students' capacities to learn independently (Willetton Senior High School, 1988). These ideas were further developed during 1989.

The Q-Centre

On Saturday, 16 June, 1990, a newspaper advertisement appeared in the professional appointments section of a morning newspaper with state-wide distribution. It contained an eye catching letter 'Q' and called for applications for a 'Q-Centre manager'. The advertisement stated:

The Q-Centre is a unique computer based learning centre about to open at Willetton. The Q-Centre will operate after hours to offer on a pay-as-you-use basis community access to the most extensive range of video and computer based training course ware currently available in the world.

Now after 3 years of planning the board of management of this exciting and innovative venture wish to appoint a Q-CENTRE MANAGER.

The successful applicant was to be 'computer literate, preferably with tuition experience and a successful track record in selling services.' The salary package was to be negotiated. Significantly, the advertisement was lodged under the aegis of Unisys and Willetton Senior High School. The school's partner, Unisys Australia Limited, was a private company which sold computers.

Not surprisingly, the advertisement also came to the attention of the Minister of Education who wanted to know more about it. As a senior official at the time, so did I. By this stage, I was generally aware of what was going on at the school but did not know the detail. In a briefing note, I was advised that the computer company was to be the employing agency and it had allocated $68,000 for personnel. I was also informed that Davies thought that 'the Minister's office' was happy with this arrangement. I sent the briefing note on to the Minister with a handwritten comment that 'Willetton is obviously a top school doing a good job.' There was more to it, however.

Over the preceding months there had been considerable traffic between the school and the Minister's office. The regulatory issues extended beyond the employment by Unisys of a manager. In a joint venture, Unisys was prepared to commit $300,000 worth of hardware and software to establish a centre at the school. In return for this investment the company would develop, in collaboration with the school, a learning system that could be marketed elsewhere. Davies and representatives of the company had met earlier with the Minister for Education and gained in-principle approval to proceed. As is often the way there was change of Minister. The new Minister was apprehensive. The Education Department did not have in place a policy regarding corporate sponsorship. The proposal raised new regulatory issues. Without an amendment to the Education Act, an agreement between a school and a company would violate legislation regarding public sector financial administration. Questions about the legality of a 'donation' of $300,000 and the disbursement of profits that might be accrued from the joint venture were also raised. Finally, after acquiring legal advice, the difficulties were resolved. The Education Department would sign the agreement on behalf of the school and the school was given the go-ahead to set up the computing centre in collaboration with the company. The end result was the same. This was a major achievement. Davies' insistence on dealing with the top, together with his persistence, paid off.

The genesis of the Q-Centre is found in the thinking of British academic Reg Revans who developed the notion of 'action learning'.[2] Revans argues that managers need not only the knowledge that comes from listening and reading but also from asking questions. It is the latter, this 'questioning insight' which is usually in short supply. The capacity to ask these questions is known as the 'Q-factor'. The Q-Centre at Willetton was named in honour of this construction of learning. Revans had corresponded with Davies during the planning and, in his nineties, visited the school in 1992. In developing his thinking Davies had also drawn on Roy Gilbert, a management consultant with public sector experience, and, Peter Hamilton, and official in the state education department. Each had played a key role in system-level policy formulation.

For readers unfamiliar with the 'etiquette' of Australian school systems, the audacity of Davies' actions should be emphasized. First, the idea that a public school, of its own initiative, might create a position and then lodge an advertisement to fill it was considered problematic. This act would have substantially eroded Davies' standing from the point of view of the officials who managed the highly-centralized staffing system. It brought him onto their turf. Second, the idea of a deal between a school and a private sector company was very unusual and potentially controversial. There were whole-of-government regulations controlling such initiatives and in general they were not encouraging. Third, the project raised basic ideological issues regarding corporate sponsorship of schools, in particular, whether such initiatives were essentially inequitable, favouring some schools ahead of others; the government of the day lacked a clear position on these issues. Finally, there was the matter of the Q-Centre itself. Hardly anyone outside of Willetton knew much about it or what it might imply. Revans' ideas had not been endorsed by the corporate executive group of the Education Department. Some of my colleagues on this body, I recall, thought the whole idea 'wacky'.

The School's Other Reforms

Even if Willetton's only reform had been the Q-Centre it would have generated controversy. However, the school embarked on various other initiatives that collectively appeared to outsiders, like me, as a form of entrepreneurial pragmatism. For example, a second key development was the establishment of an academy for young women which critics described as a kind of finishing school in which students learned 'grooming and deportment'. Its aim, at its inception, was to prepare female students for secretarial and management positions in the business world though in subsequent years its focus broadened and male students were included in the program. The scheme was guaranteed to raise the hackles of the strong feminist lobby in the education bureaucracy; Davies and his program were perceived to be sexist. The program became the subject of gossip. I recall discussing the program with Davies. Pragmatic as always, he explained that 'this is what industry wants'. Often apparently insignificant social skills, such as being confident enough to look an employer in the eye during an interview, made the difference between getting a job or a knock-back. He also saw it as a way of competing with the private schools whose students were often advantaged in these respects. The academy's program was overseen by a board of successful business women.

Sometimes, it is the apparently minor details that turn out to be most problematic. Davies engaged one of the school's secretarial staff members to coordinate the program, a person with wide secretarial experience though without formal teaching qualifications. This innovation, Davies argued, was in keeping with a general trend towards blurring the boundaries between professional and non-professional roles.[3] Davies took the position that if a school were to become a learning community then all members of that community should be involved, where possible, in teaching and learning. Who better to teach young women about the social nous they require in the business world than a capable and experienced secretary? Members of the wider school community became involved in school matters that had previously been the sole preserve of teachers. His rhetoric matched that of Laurie Carmichael a unionist with a national profile who visited the school during this period.[4] Many people wondered how a state high school had managed to attract such a celebrity.

Davies' third change, the internal restructuring of senior positions (the flattened structure, he called it), brought the union into the school. The standard is for senior school positions, including that of principal, to be filled without any decisive input from schools or their communities. Once appointed, incumbents can stay in their positions until they retire unless their school is 're-classified' which is a bureaucratic process.[5] Staff may elect to transfer though they are rarely transferred against their will. The consequence of this policy is that it maintains the stability of standard school programs. The rule systems that the school adopts usually preclude any major self-introduced restructuring. Incumbents, including principals, deputies and heads of departments occupy established roles. Because of the centralized staffing procedures, Davies was unable to fill these senior positions with persons who shared his convictions so he created a parallel structure and filled the positions with staff members sympathetic to the emerging reform program. The incumbents would have been considered by human resources bureaucrats to be teachers with additional duties and an allowance not as administrators occupying formal promotional positions. Several of those who held administrative positions formally recognized by the central office were not part of the new 'cabinet'. They watched while their responsibilities and power were taken from them and, understandably, felt marginalized as the school came to operate according to these new rule systems.

The fourth of the school's initiatives was as controversial as the others. Willetton sought to exploit a policy of relaxing zoning regulations so that parents who lived outside gazetted school boundaries might exercise some choice of schooling for their children. This policy was necessary in order to support another policy of 'curriculum specialization' whereby schools were encouraged to develop areas of excellence in fields such as art, music, technology and science. Officials reluctantly introduced the new policy because they feared that should they be too permissive they might be inadvertently opening the floodgates of boundary crossing. This would make the life of central planners and resource managers exponentially more difficult. It might also lead to discerning parents deserting neighbourhood schools and contributing to the growth of a small number of elite public schools. If 'elite' meant 'excellent' then Willetton sought to become an elite school and competed for students from outside the nominated boundaries.

Governments have to balance principles. On the one hand they have in recent times favoured extending choice, on the other they have promoted the values of efficiency and effectiveness. On the surface it appears that these principles can be compatible but, in Willetton's case, they came into conflict. As Willetton's numbers escalated to make it the largest school in the state, neighbouring schools experienced concomitant depletions in student numbers. For these schools this meant not only under-utilized facilities but also fewer staff and the prospect of having to narrow curriculum offerings.

Willetton's school council, understanding that the squeaky wheel gets the grease, convened public meetings with huge attendances to promote its need for new buildings. As a result, questions came to be asked about how the student population had burgeoned to the extend that it had. As long as parents had a residential address in an appropriate area then parents were entitled to enrol a child at a particular school. It was said not only of Willetton, but also of other schools, that parents nominally re-located in order to comply with that policy. Willetton's enrolment practices were put under the microscope in a way which Davies argues was unfair because there was no comparison made with the enrolment practices of schools with diminishing numbers. A union official told me that the union executive had received messages of concern that Willetton had been offering scholarships for students from outside the district that were not really scholarships, but were really a way of boosting numbers. I have no information about whether smaller schools guilty of this also drew attention for what was a fairly common practice.

In these ventures the school worked on the edge of what was legal and what was not. They were careful to avoid blatantly breaking the rules though they were continually questioning of them. Davies and his supporters took the philosophy of action learning seriously. They saw their job as that of 'the Q-factor manager [who] will question rules, regulations, programs and procedures and change them if they do not make sense'.[6] This approach was not greatly different from that recommended by most of the senior union and departmental executives I interviewed; these leaders did not report feeling bound to slavishly follow rules.

Exclusion from the National Schools Project

Willetton did not participate in the National Schools Project. For a start Davies and his school team were ambivalent about joining. They feared that this would lead them to fall under the control of outsiders. Further, they had been involved in restructuring well before the National Schools Project had been dreamed up. They knew what they wanted whereas most of the pilot schools had only begun to think about restructuring issues.

The Project's Education Department representatives wanted Willetton to participate because it was already pushing the regulatory limits. Others in the Education Department who were not associated with the Project, I recall, were less enthusiastic about this; to them Willetton was a trouble-making school because of the unwillingness of its principal to 'play by the rules'. Their view was that if Willetton was a prototype pilot school, then the whole question of participating in reform projects ought to be reviewed. The school became for many of my colleagues the reification of the Government's devolution reforms: borderline anarchy. This is what could be expected 800 times over if the reforms came to fruition. Ultimately, however, the teachers' union's opposition became the sticking point.

According to a member of the union's executive committee, his colleagues on the executive were ambivalent about incorporating Willetton in the Project. Part of the opposition sprang from a perception of teachers being oppressed by an insensitive administration. On the other hand, the view was put to the executive that it would be easier to control the school if it were a member. There were informal discussions at the school between Davies and Project representatives; subsequently, union and department representatives jointly addressed a meeting, attended by most of the 100 or so staff, to explain the purposes of the Project and the implications of joining. However, nothing came of the meeting. 'I never ever felt that Brendon [Davies] understood what we were talking about,' the union official who spoke at the meeting told me. Davies wanted support from the Project for what he was already doing or had in mind. He saw no point in subjecting his staff to the introductory courses undertaken by staff in other pilot schools. My union friend lamented Davies' attitude, 'Well, I've got a few projects. Are you prepared to support them?', was how he represented it. This was not acceptable to the unionist. 'We never engaged. It's almost as if we were talking foreign languages to one another', he said.

Balancing Support and Opposition

Departmental Officials

Davies avoided the line management inherent in the departmental bureaucracy. When he wanted departmental support he preferred to go to the top. He believed that if he could get an okay from the Minister or a senior official or a member of the department's executive group, then decisions made at these levels would filter down to his immediate supervisors. 'He was like an unstoppable freight train,' a former director said to me. 'There was no mechanism for having a proper conversation with him.'

He was also a salesman wanting to get to 'yes' as quickly as possible. Davies would make an appointment and turn up with key members of his team. They would table some documentation and then ask for help. What they wanted to do nearly always tested the limits of some policy or regulation. If he had started at the bottom and tried to work up through line management he would have been stymied well before he got to officials with the power to say 'yes'. I could see why middle management would find it all too hard. Davies was also politically active and networked quite openly with local politicians on both sides of parliament, selling to them his vision for the school. He had no hesitation in writing directly to the Minister of Education or the State Premier if he thought it would help his cause. He was never reprimanded for doing so, either.

Davies, on his own admission, was no saint. Colleagues also had misgivings, some stronger than mine, about the approach being taken by the school. One superintendent at the time believed that the school's curriculum philosophy was too populist and not sufficiently based on educational principles. A lot of what needed to be taught might not necessarily be what the students or their parents wanted in the curriculum. The girls' academy, for example, was highly controversial. Teaching 'make up' seemed way out of line. 'You don't teach creation science in schools because it's popular among a particular group of parents,' the former superintendent said. 'What they were doing wasn't consistent with the philosophy of national curriculum statements.[7] 'I was under pressure to stomp on him,' my colleague reported, 'but I felt ambivalent towards what the school overall was doing so I left him alone.'

While still a bureaucrat, I was sceptical about some of what Davies and his colleagues had put in place but took the position that the purpose of devolution policies was to allow those working in schools to decide what needed to be changed instead of officials imposing their favourite innovations on schools. And there was so much grumbling among so many of Davies' fellow principals about how hard it all was, how they needed more staff, more time, more of everything that, by comparison, I felt Willetton was a breath of fresh air. I used to refer to the school as an exemplar of the initiative that was possible under the devolution reforms. I wore a t-shirt Davies sent me with pride; it had a 'Q' logo on the front and the equation 'L=P+Q' on the back. This represented Reg Revans' theory; Learning equals Programs and Questioning.

Union Officials

Some union leaders saw Willetton as the thin edge of the wedge. The side-lining of administrators in official promotional positions was a first step towards the dismantling of the centralized staffing system and its replacement with local selection of staff. From the first whiff that the government intended to introduce local staff selection, the union had drawn the line; it would not allow local selection under any circumstances. Staff displaced by the new

Willetton decision-making structures complained to the union and sought to enlist its support. Though Davies and the majority of the Willetton staff were union members, and though the majority supported the changes, the larger union interest was to come first as far as the leadership was concerned.

The union saw the Willetton reforms occurring without attention to 'due process'. Complaints from members at the school suggested that it was being ruled by 'grace and favour'. The complainants felt that they were not consulted. 'We were supposed to have participatory decision making but there didn't seem to be much of that unless you were within a three metre radius of Brendon when the decisions were made,' I was told by a union official. What he thought was necessary was the formation of a whole school view that 'allowed a divergent view to be accommodated in the process.' This was the process formally adopted by pilot schools in which the union had a voice. It certainly curbed impetuous decision making by the principal. Davies, however, was not against putting proposals to the vote and risking the possibility of losing. On a number of occasions he did this and lost. However, as far as he was concerned, if a change was supported by 80 or 90 percent of the staff, then he had a mandate to proceed.

Collegial Support

Davies did not invest any effort in cultivating the support of other school principals. He had little time for the professional association of high school principals and was seen by many of its members as a maverick. He was a newcomer to their ranks: Willetton was only his second principalship. He did not fit their model of an outstanding principal.[8]

Davies' attitude towards enrolment did not foster his relationship with other principals. 'He was being predatory on [the students of] neighbouring schools,' a colleague put it. 'A lot of them just despised Brendon,' another told me. 'But it's basically because he got up there and told them "You're too bloody lazy, your schools are boring, you've basically retired in your school." And I mean, a lot of those old blokes used to hate that. So a lot of it was envy in a way.' In addition, they resented Davies' practice of 'going straight to the top'. Other principals saw this as a form of queue jumping. The system would collapse if all principals pushed their way into executive directors' offices to sell their pet projects.

The Community

The most important source of support (power) came from Davies' ties to the local community. Willetton is a comfortable, leafy suburb of the kind favoured by small business owners who believe in the work ethic. During its early years the school, which had been seen as a systemic alternative school in the seventies, drew public attention for its practice of allowing students to address staff on a first-name basis. 'Warm, friendly and open teacher–student relationships' were emphasized. The school was one of the first in the state to employ a school chaplain. Davies took the school in another direction. He emphasized dress codes. Students were to wear uniforms. Staff were expected to dress formally. A colleague reported to me how, while visiting the school, he witnessed a prospective staff member on a first visit being ticked off for wearing casual dress. In these respects, the school modelled itself on private school traditions.

Davies approached his role in the school the way a company chief executive would approach the board, the shareholders, the employees and the customers. This might have been how private school principals saw their jobs but it was a radical construction of the role of a public school principal. Through the parent leaders on the board and his low-key use of a persuasive vernacular, he could mobilize huge numbers of parents to support some initiative the school was taking. From the outside it appeared to be a masterful demonstration of community support and superintendents and other officials who confronted it were initially flummoxed by the display of power at public meetings.

Coming Unstuck: The Official Intervention

In 1994, several years after I had left the Education Department I received a visit from two former colleagues who wanted to talk to me about Willetton and its principal. I was not sure whether this was an official visit or 'off the record'. It turned out that they were acting on the instructions of the head of the Education Department and were undertaking an audit of the school which was purported to be in some kind of serious trouble. I quickly felt defensive not only of Davies but also of my own actions. My visitors seemed to imply that if Davies had undergone adequate training in financial management, or if he had been restrained from proceeding so far so fast, the current difficulties could have been averted. This argument had often been thrown at me when I was responsible for the implementation of the devolution reforms some years earlier. It seemed to me if the argument were taken too literally, then substantial reform would never happen. Everyone would be required to proceed at the same pedestrian rate. It was an argument used to keep everyone in tow. Training can become a means of central control.

As the meeting progressed it became clear that Davies was in some kind of trouble. The exact details were not revealed but the concern of the visitors had to do with financial management. They implied that the paperwork was not in order. Neither Davies nor his staff were under any suspicion of wrong doing, they explained to me though, as the principal, Davies was accountable for managing the school's finances and the Regulations were quite clear about how this was to be done. After the meeting I felt quite alarmed. Auditors could inspect the books of just about any high school and find something to complain about given that the handbook on school financial management is 520 pages long. The probability of doing so was obviously going to be higher in a school that was engaged in fund raising and joint ventures, though as Davies later pointed out to me, three months prior to the intervention the school had undergone a routine external audit and received an excellent report. Subsequent audits of the school described the school's financial management as exemplary.

Nevertheless, the state's most senior education bureaucrat had explicitly instructed Davies to assist with the investigation and comply with the directions of the district superintendent. A senior official and an auditor from the cental office were 'installed' in the school to 'sort things out'. The school was to be firmly re-instated in the line management structure. Davies complied. 'We're a bureaucratic school now,' he told me recently. 'We do all the right things. The school's now driving with the handbrake half on.'

When I spoke with a senior official, he assured me the audit of the school occurred because of an official complaint which had to be followed up and had nothing to do with the school's history of independent action. He refused to expand. Nevertheless, it was clear that Davies was being given no option but to comply; the alternative was dismissal. In my discussions with colleagues who had been supporters of the school there was a sense of pessimism, a realization that this intervention had symbolic as well as legal significance. It was time to clip Davies' wings and signal to the others that a more moderate response was now required.

The particular act or circumstance that triggered the intervention remains a mystery to Davies. Some disaffected staff members had written to the Education Department complaining about the school administration, but there was no precedent in the school system for such a full-blooded audit arising from the complaints by staff. Presumably, if an isolated instance of concern had been raised it could have been investigated by a more routine procedure than one in which a senior officer and an auditor were ensconced in the school for a period of three months.

Davies reports that the Education Department's head had told him that this was something that had to be done and that no harm would come to him. Supporters of the school in the central office were given a similar message: 'Just keep your head down until its over. It's going to be messy but Brendon shouldn't get hurt'. It seemed that the school had to be taught a lesson though the reason was not officially disclosed.

The Broken Meta-rules

The texts of official rules that in some way or other were used by the players at Willetton can be easily perused. They are artefacts. The meta-rules cannot so easily be defined. They were woven into the discourse which situated the principal and his staff in power relationships with officials from the Education Department and teachers' union. The discourse which governed these relations sometimes alludes to the official rules and sometimes to an informal though publicly stated understanding. It is also governed by rules of the game that cannot be held up to the light to be examined because they are implicit. Despite the limitations this creates, I consider my own experience and association with Willetton school together with interviews with employer and union officials to be sufficient to explicate the meta-rules in operation.

The first meta-rule that Davies broke was one which requires that the pain and benefits of change should be shared around equally.[9] Kudos is one of the benefits. Although not unaware of the importance of paying attention to stakeholders, ultimately Davies was unable to accommodate everyone and at the same time maintain the integrity of the reforms he introduced. The more prominent the success of the school the greater the chagrin of those who had been sidelined or made to feel redundant. The administrators who were stripped of traditional roles and union members who did not support the restructuring reported being marginalized. Central office bureaucrats had been circumvented. The teacher union leaders were threatened by the way local politicians were courted by Davies without reference to them. And principals of neighbouring schools felt envious as they watched resources stream into the school as a result of burgeoning student numbers. Traditional opponents joined forces and through informal networks were able to undermine the changes on the basis that they were unfair — unfair to staff at the school, unfair to other schools and unfair to students outside the school.

The second meta-rule Davies broke was one which dictates that people should know their place and enlist the cooperation of those with power from their positions as subordinates.[10] Davies' strategy of going to the top was successful initially. He was well placed to cooperate with those in power when the education system's leaders were reformist. However, he was stranded when reform itself came to be defined as a problem, rather than as a solution to other problems, as occurred after a change of government. By this stage, Davies was seen to be someone who did not know his place nor understand that a new government meant new policies. Instead of being able to go straight to the top, Davies was forced to go back to the middle managers he had formerly scorned. Ironically, the new policies promoted more traditional relationships between principals and their superordinates.

The third meta-rule which Davies broke was one which requires public sector administrators to match their program to the resources available, not the other way around.[11] It is generally considered impractical to assess what programs are needed first and then seek to attract the resources needed to provide them because of the risks of identifying needs which cannot be met.

In some regards Davies was very successful at attracting resources by using the standard procedures which apply to schools. Most resources are tied to student numbers so he attracted staff and financial grants proportionate to the number of students enrolled. However, because of his success, the school was not able to house all the students attracted to it. The parents lobbied for more infrastructure which would not only have been a major cost but would be wasted if, in fact, it were the principal's leadership which was attracting students. Should Davies transfer or retire the school could be left with under-utilized buildings as was already the case in a number of surrounding schools. For a principal's leadership style to result in an increased need for infrastructure expenditure placed extraordinary demands on the system. School building programs were planned years in advance on the basis of demographic trends, not consumer demand. It was another case of redefining the problem. Instead of low levels of consumer satisfaction being a problem which needed to be addressed, consumer satisfaction created problems because it led to demands for substantial unplanned expenditure.

Davies broke a fourth meta-rule by drawing attention to problems instead of successes. He did this by adopting a demeanour which instead of obfuscating activities that were problematic either for himself or for others, drew attention to them. This occurred, in part, because he used colloquial language in such a way that if you were not for him you were against him. Critics were 'dinosaurs'. He was fond of slogans such as 'We've divorced the Education Department and married industry'. Supporters found the language witty or funny. Opponents thought it intemperate, even seditious. This directness was incompatible with the emerging importance attached to public relations in the public sector. Publicists were paid to represent education systems in terms of an ideal: a benign central office lightly managing a system of enlightened schools. Davies' language tended to position him outside the system, and irrespective of whatever good work he and his colleagues might have been doing, incited some form of intervention.

As discussed in Chapter 7, school principals have substantial freedom within a highly regulated system providing they do not provoke an official complaint and providing they are not perceived to be testing the authority of senior officials. The art of school leadership, in such a system, is to avoid representing what the school is doing in such a way that others perceive it to be a problem which they are obliged to act upon. Davies' forthrightness, led officials to perceive a highly successful school as highly problematic.

Conclusion

Six years have passed since the lodging of the advertisement for the Q-Centre. Davies is still the principal and 'doing a good job' according to a senior official. As I write, Willetton has been praised publicly by the Education Minister as a school 'able to maintain one of the State's top academic records' (Reardon, 1996). The Q-Centre, or the 'Reg Revans Complex' as it is now known, is still there though the out-of-hours adult education program has ceased. The academy for girls has been wound up. The school is managed within the standard hierarchical structures that reflect the career structure of the wider school system. Set aside the question of whether the changes at Willetton have been improvements; I have not sought to answer it. I have no way of knowing. The point of this story is that the school was being propelled along a trajectory that was taking it out of the orbit of the public education system. It has now been brought under control.

This has been an abbreviated account of a complex story that deserves a more complete telling. I hope it is not a caricature. I am conscious in writing my account, which encapsulates years of struggle involving hundreds of teachers and officials, of the process of simplification. It may seem from my account transparently obvious where things went wrong. 'They went too fast', 'They should have consolidated', 'They should have kept the union on-side' were comments reported to me. Yet if the school had followed the conventional wisdom about how to proceed it would never have challenged the authorized versions of what was good and what was allowable. There is a school reform discourse, reflected in the National Schools Project, for example, which legitimizes the purpose of reform and how it should be accomplished and which, in its own way, imposes limits and boundaries around what is desirable and permissible. This discourse values gradualism, working from the bottom upwards, promoting a teacher's eye view of what could and should be changed. While it may encourage better schools, improvement is defined in terms of the confines of 'the mould' defined by this discourse. Davies rejected this construction of reform.

From the beginning of his term as Principal, Davies and his colleagues worked in the penumbra of the regulatory system. Many of the changes they sought were neither clearly legal nor illegal within the existing regulatory framework. In coming to, 'Yes', officials need to exercise discretion and the school leaders to take risks. This is the grey zone within which regulatory reform takes place. It is also the 'zone' where, in the face of ambiguity and uncertainty, meta-rules commonly come into play. Had the starting point of the Willetton reforms been strict adherence to the meta-rules, insofar as they could have been articulated publicly at that time, it is doubtful that Davies could have implemented many of the projects that were later put into effect. For example, in order to satisfy all the stake-holders the agenda would have had to have been considerably watered down. It is easier and safer to comply with the meta-rules but the price of conformity and safety is the perpetuation of normalcy.

Eventually, the official rules were used to return Willetton to the systemic fold. The bureaucracy had the power and the means to do so. The intention was not to nullify the school's capacity to be innovative because that quality, in some senses, is valued. 'We don't want all this terrific stuff to stop,' Davies was told by one of the officials sent to 'fix the school up'. Rather, the intention was to require the school to work within the meta-rules that enable officials to make the system appear manageable, that is, keep the various parts in their place.

I spoke off the record to a number of individuals currently holding positions as officials in the Education Department. They took pains to emphasize that the official audit of the school did not reveal any wrong doing on Davies' part. They spoke approvingly of his character. They regretted the crisis but argued emphatically that intervention was in the school's interest and the public interest. Other schools needed to learn from Willetton's lesson as they made their way towards self-management.

I am reminded by Willetton of Jeffrey Mirel's account of Bensenville, the school that would 'break the mould'. The Bensenville experiment never got off the ground. Davies and his team flew with Willetton for six or more years before crash-landing. In the period 1991–3, the school soared, by most accounts, even by the somewhat grudging accounts of its critics. This seems to be the story of most extraordinary schools.

Notes

1   This was known as the Managing Change in Schools Project and was a forerunner to the National Schools Project.
2   See Roy Gilbert, *Reglomania*, pp. 5–6.
3   This view was encapsulated in 'award restructuring', an approach to industrial relations reform being promoted by the Australian Council of Trade Unions and the Federal Government.
4   Laurie Carmichael, as former Assistant Secretary of the Australian Council of Trade Unions, was a principal architect of award restructuring.
5   Schools are classified according to size for administrative reasons. The effect of this is to require principals to transfer when student numbers change significantly. No discrimination is made between fluctuations which result from the leadership qualities of principals and those resulting from demographic changes. The only reason Davies was not required to transfer when student numbers increased so significantly at Willetton was that the school was already in the top category.
6   Roy Gilbert, *Reglomania*, p. 6.
7   A statement about national curriculum goals, *Common and Agreed National Goals for Schooling in Australia*, Melbourne: Australian Education Council, 1989, implies the legitimacy of some approaches to equity over others.
8   He is *not* among the ten principals featured in a departmental publication *Principals: In Pursuit of Excellence*, Perth: Ministry of Education, 1990. In the preface, the Director General at the time wrote: 'Readers will not be surprised to see the importance these principals place on communication and on the relationship between schools and their communities.' p. (i) Among the principals featured is Davies' predecessor at Willetton, who describes the qualities required for the job. 'Above all,' he presciently writes 'he [the principal] must not buckle under pressure.' p. 29.
9   This bears some resemblance to the 'Something for everyone' operational principle suggested by Marshall, Mitchell and Wirt in *Culture and Education Policy in the American States*, p. 44.
10 This meta-rule is related to Burns and Flam's meta-rules of compliance, *the Shaping of Social Organization*, pp. 217–18. It is also similar to the 'Know your place

and cooperate with those in power' operational principle proposed by Marshall, Mitchell and Wirt, p. 43.

11   This is similar to the operational policy, 'State resources drive policy', found in Marshall, Mitchell and Wirt, p. 48 except that they specifically refer to policies. The meta-rule I propose here is broader in scope; it comes from a value that good public sector employees only spend within allocations made and never ask for more than has already been allocated.

10 The Rules of School Reform

You must know, then, that there are two methods of fighting, one by law, the other by force: the first method is that of men, the second of beasts; but as the first method is often insufficient, one must have recourse to the second . . . A prince must know how to use both natures, and that the one without the other is not durable. (Machiavelli)

Introduction

In this final chapter, I draw the argument together and suggest how it can be used to reframe thinking about school reform. Before beginning, however, I will restate two of the suppositions that underpin my argument.

First, it is important to remember that I am not arguing that there has been no lasting change to schooling over the past century. Rather, I have sought to explain why certain patterns of classroom instruction have persisted in the face of concerted effort to change them. I acknowledge that some features of schools have changed. It would be fatuous to argue otherwise. The curriculum is obviously different in various respects. The proportion of students continuing their schooling beyond the age at which attendance is compulsory has increased. There are fewer one-teacher schools. Central bureaucracies are larger. The initial training of teachers is more extensive. It is easy to catalogue differences. But the basic forms of teaching have endured. Whole class teaching is typical. The day is scheduled into periods. Teacher talk predominates. Though there may be noticeable differences, there are also many constants.

Second, I have argued my case from a systemic perspective, having in mind collectivities of schools that are legally under the control of central education authorities. I recognize that there are individual schools that make their own rules and in which work is organized on radically different bases to the conventional school as we know it. Some of these innovative schools function within — they may even be sponsored by — larger school systems; others are private and are largely independent of federal, state or regional governments on operational matters. However, such schools are relatively few in number and can be expected, over an extended period of time, to revert to more conventional patterns of school organization. Sometimes, in the public education system, these schools are 'show cases' and there is seldom any sustained attempt to convert all the schools in the system to the new patterns on display. I have in mind Deborah Meier's (1995) famous school, Central Part East, in

New York. Such schools provide icons within the public sector and inspire teachers and others who visit and read about it. However, inspiration is not enough to shift systemic regulatory controls. Concerted efforts towards mass conversion to new forms of teaching and work organization have failed to take effect. In this book, I am less interested in explaining the internal dynamics of exceptional schools than in explaining why so little of the exceptional quality rubs off, or outlasts the generation of teachers who created it. I do not claim to have the complete answer to why this is so, however, I am convinced that the interplay of rules is one part of it.

A Regulatory Perspective on School Reform

Looking at schools from a perspective where all aspects of regulation are considered reframes school reform in a number of respects. First, the labels that are commonly applied to different kinds of school reform, labels such as 'school-based decision-making', 'waivers', 'restructuring', 'top–down', 'devolution', and so on can no longer be considered reliable. These are too approximate. It is more helpful to describe the reform in terms of the nature and extent of the regulatory adjustments that are being made rather than use this limited short-hand. Approval to redesign the school's governance in toto constitutes a quite different kind of reform than one where a school is exempted from a few minor rules even though both could crudely be classified as examples of 'waivers'.

Second, reform itself is constructed as a form of re-regulation. Educational reform inevitably involves the adoption of new rules, official and informal. In most cases the official rules are few in number and, relative to the corpus of rules already in place, constitute a very small proportion. However, school reform is not simply a matter of deleting a few old rules from a list and promulgating the new ones. Because, in practice, the already existing official rules are combined with informal rules into systems of rules they are hard to pull apart and reassemble, irrespective of whether you are the head of a state department of education or an enterprising teacher. There are two reasons why this is so. First, once a rule has been 'normalized', that is, become part of the taken-for-granted activities of the organization, it is largely out of the control of the officials who promulgated it. The other reason is that the official rule becomes part of an interconnected system of rules; it may not be possible to expunge part of the system and keep the routine of activities going that the system supports. This may seem self-evident but for some reasons it is consistently overlooked in considerations of school reform.

Third, the tendency to construe reform as policy makers often describe it — Reform achieved by Regulation — as though what is imagined in the board room of the central authority represents what actually happens in schools is brought into question. School reform, for those doing it, is not some special activity that can be partitioned from the day-to-day activities that occur during a typical work day. 'It's 9.30 a.m. so I'll do school reform for half an hour.' Whatever the changes required to implement the reform, they have to be fitted into a tightly woven set of existing practices. Some of these informal rules may seem quite trivial and therefore bound to give way under the pressure of the 'Big R' regulatory changes but the analogy of Gulliver struggling to throw off his thread-like bonds is apposite. Rules apparently unrelated to the reform, often about routine matters, for example, students not being permitted in class-rooms unless supervised by a teacher, turn out to be crucially important. All of these informal and formal rules 'make the classroom' and suggest to those who occupy it how the activities that occur within it are meant to proceed. This is why, as Michael Kirst and Gail Meister (1985) observe, additive reforms rather than fundamental restructuring have the better prospect of succeeding. For example, in order to achieve a new curriculum objective, it is easier to reify the objective into a new subject and form a new subject department in a high school than to orient the whole of the school's curriculum towards achieving the objective. 'Self-contained' reforms, with separate, internal rule regimes, leave the larger system of rules relatively unchanged.

I can understand why informal rules which shape the response of particip-ants to the reform are ignored by officials making policy. Most of these rules are unwritten and some are unspoken. How would a policy maker even know how they operated? Not surprisingly, therefore, such rules are rarely acknow-ledged in any calculation about how to implement the reform or in any post-mortem of the reform's implementation other than under the general rubric of 'culture'. Officials who devise the reform have no control over these rules and, because they are seldom documented and often subject to local variations, are inclined to dismiss them.

Finally, I have shown that reform can be obstructed by rules that on the surface seem unrelated to, or several steps removed from, the objective of the reform. The official rules that may constrain reform are therefore not always obvious.

I am not contending that this is the only, or necessarily best, way to frame school reform. However, it is a perspective that for the most part has been unused. Reformers change rules, but not always with foreknowledge of the effects.

The Official Rules and School Governance

Are the official rules a key steering mechanism in the governance of schools? The answer to this question is a qualified 'yes'. I have alluded to the answer previously and will now bring the pieces of the argument together.

The first part of the argument concerns knowledge of the official rules. There seems to be ample evidence that teachers know what to do but do not have a first-hand knowledge of the official rules. However, they want to operate according to the rules, or to put it slightly differently, they do not want to work outside them. Teachers are like other members of the public in this regard. They respect the law and want to follow it because they think they should.[1] The way they routinely determine their position is not by referring to the rule book, metaphorically speaking, but by following the example of others, fitting into established work patterns, and accepting direction from immediate supervisors.

With regard to the officials, with relatively few exceptions, they do not know if the rules are being observed or not. In most cases they do not need to know. The operations of a school system can be likened to a sporting contest from the officials' point of view. Their job is to keep the game flowing; they are the umpires. The players and spectators know the game and rarely think about the formal rules of the game. As long as the game is being played in the right spirit, the officials and players are content to ignore minor infractions of the rules. If this did not happen, and the umpires were officious or the players continually appealed against an opponent's infringement of a rule, the game could not be played to anyone's satisfaction. The rules, therefore, define the game as much as restrict it. Thus, most of the rules are not strictly invigilated because to do so would spoil the game, or in the case of schools, interfere with a shared understanding of how schools should operate. There is usually no need for the invigilation.

This is not the same as stating that there are no rules or that there is no need for rules. To continue with the sporting metaphor, the game depends on the rules and some knowledge of them by players, spectators and umpires. If someone proposed to abandon the rules because they were not needed there would be massive resistance.

Of course school systems are not the same as sporting events. And some rules are more important than others. Although central education authorities usually retain the power to set the rules they do not have the means to invigilate most of them. They will, however, do their best to invigilate rules that provide a basis for their power, that is, they will respond to direct challenges to any aspect of these rules. These are the rules which authorize them to reward and punish employees; these are kept in good working order even if they are rarely used. And they will invigilate the rules that are contained in awards and contracts since that is a field of ongoing contestation between union and departmental officials and needs to be closely watched. Matters to do with school finance will be closely examined since there is a strong public interest in the outcome; also there are trained auditors to help with the watching. Rules that govern the careers of employees and their salaries will also be kept under scrutiny by their employees themselves and their union representatives. These rules are invigilated because they have strategic importance for the formation and maintenance of power relationships.

In conjunction with this relatively small collection of 'important' rules, policies, as distinct from rules connected to legislative processes, are used to publicly steer the school system. These steering policies rarely make reference to existing rules and regulations which are more like ballast. The legal bases of these policy statements are *assumed* to exist, though more so it would seem in Australia than in the United States. Usually, however, the policies are issued under general administrative powers delegated to senior officials. Official rules may come into play if there is a complaint about someone's performance arising from mishap, incompetence or disobedience in relation to the implementation of the policy and it becomes necessary, after the fact, to see whether the complaint can be justified in terms of an infringement of the rules.

There are few explicit rules about how to teach though teaching is *de facto* regulated as a result of the accumulation of rules that encase, and so shape, work organization. As I explained, in regard to Lundgren's frame factor theory these work organization rules can have a powerful impact on micropedagogical processes even though it was not devised with this intention. However, teachers and officials do not generally feel restricted by this level of regulation. They are content with the possibilities which they perceive to exist within the regulatory framework. Many are also able to recognize that some aspects of the limitations provided also serve a protective function.

So far, in my argument, the official rules have been presented in benign rather than malevolent terms. This is not the end of the argument. I maintain that rules are an integral part of the system of control and system maintenance but the way this happens is not through the force of individual rules but through systems of rules.

The Nexus Between Rules and Reform

I have described how many of the current school reform efforts are being engineered by deregulating aspects of schooling. In most cases of deregulation, where selected rules are waived or abolished, the power of central authorities is left legally and symbolically undiminished. Giving *permission* to do something is not, by my definition, giving power no matter how collegial and warm the relationship within which it is given. In some cases, waiving or shedding rules may actually strengthen central controls since the act of exemption or abolition is a tangible, public reminder of the power of central authorities.

Thus reform begins under the aegis of the official rules. In some organizations the rules may have been severely culled but they are never completely discarded. In whatever form they exist they have a general symbolic significance in addition to constraining actions and limiting options and sometimes even providing specific direction. They legitimate the power of persons in positions of authority. They create the semblance of rational, bureaucratic governance. Their existence ensures a pliancy in the relationship between supervisor and subordinate.

If teachers are satisfied that their employer is acting in their interest there is no need to be constantly checking to see that new policies are within the legal limits prescribed by the appropriate statutes. A similar relationship might exist between teachers and unions which may also be seen as acting on behalf of teachers. A kind of treaty is put in place which, in effect, says, 'If we can see that you are representing our interests we won't hassle you' (see Powell *et al.*, 1985). From the teachers' perspective, having an employer or union look after your interests frees you to focus attention on the matters that are of immediate concern in the classroom and, perhaps, the larger school environment. Referral to rules under these circumstances seems legalistic. From the officials' perspective this mutual understanding of the limits allows them to get on with other facets of their jobs. I am not suggesting that such deals are unprincipled. In my experience, officials saw themselves working diligently in the interests of not always appreciative teachers. But it left them in their corporate headquarters unchallenged by teachers and in control of their sphere of operation and teachers in control of theirs.

This equilibrium can be threatened by school reforms, particularly when they introduce uncertainty into the relationship between officials and teachers. This is where meta-rules come into play. When there is a conflict arising from a new, official rule, or a new regime of rules, introduced as part of a reform program, actors draw on meta-rules to resolve the conflict or reduce the uncertainty. The meta-rules are the real organizers. They span the rule regimes and informal rule systems. They bridge discrepancy. They keep the administrative system intact. The meta-rules are learned deductively by watching how people in school systems behave and listening to instructive stories in such a way that a shared understanding can exist without them needing to be made explicit. The meta-rules are held in place by power relations evident in the discourses of the school system and supported by the official rules. To change the meta-rules would require changing the power relations. Reformers who are unable to change the power relations, but nevertheless press ahead with their reform and 'break the mould', in so doing break meta-rules and bear the consequences. The case of Willetton describes how this happens.

In discussions with senior officials on both the employer and union sides, the majority expressed a commitment to reform of some kind or other. Yet even with their power, their control of the regulatory system and a discourse which places them in an apparently commanding position in relation to their employees, they cannot achieve what they want. This is because they do not create the meta-rules: they are at the same time positioned and constrained by them.

Senior officials are not all-powerful. The authority of senior officials is accepted by others providing that they operate within the shared expectancies of what officials can and should do. Were they to exceed these expectancies and seek to impose their own ideas about how schools should operate in a way that challenged the meta-rules then they could expect to be resisted and eventually drawn back into line.

Explaining the National Schools Project

Throughout the book, I have alluded to the Australian National Schools Project. In this section, I synthesize the aspects of my argument which relate to it.

There are several parts to the 'official' explanation of why there was no need at the end of the National Schools Project to review the regulatory framework. One is that the culture of the schools produced a 'mind-set' among staff, limiting their assessment of what needed to change and what could be changed in their school. Culture rather than regulation was the main problem. Another is that the official regulations literally did not restrict the adoption of new forms of school organization and pedagogy because, after all, they contained few explicit references to teaching. Therefore, it was argued, there was no need to recast the regulations to improve teaching. In terms of my earlier metaphor, attention shifted from the shell to the mollusc inside. It was too difficult to consider each in relation to the other.

There is an alternative explanation. I contend that the shell of work organization rules that frame teaching were placed out of reach of the pilot schools. The preservation of these rules served the interests of centralized union and school administrations. Even though one side would like to have changed some of the work organization regulations held dear by the other, neither wanted the whole regulatory edifice to collapse on them. For this reason both unions and education departments had no intention of devolving power to schools, nor saw any need to do so. Attempts to establish a Project steering group with strong pilot school representation were rejected. The officials saw themselves as the appointed or elected representatives of teachers, better able to fathom from their 'big picture' analyses what was in their constituents' interests. This belief was played out in various ways. Central authorities, unions and education departments alike, believed that there could be advantages in privately exempting a school from a rule than going through the formal process established for the Project. An even better solution would be to find a way of supporting a school which would avoid altogether a challenge to an official rule. Teachers knew that they were more likely to get what they wanted by working in this way with the union and department authorities.

The Project produced competing rhetorics; the employers represented the interests of the government and line management in the school systems; unions promoted the rhetoric of professionalism in which teacher union officials were represented as serving the interests of 'the common teacher'. Participants in schools realized — they could read between the lines — that the official rhetoric of the Project should not be taken literally. An unwritten objective of the pilot schools was to find out what their employer and their unions wanted from the Project and, where each wanted different outcomes, to situate themselves in the middle, though more closely toward the party which they presumed held the balance of power. Usually this was the teacher union because the union had a stronger presence in most of the Project schools. The equilibrium was maintained by the meta-rule that schools should know their place and, therefore, not challenge publicly the rules of the Project. Teachers who sought to reconcile their position in relation to these competing rhetorics were able to do so by going through informal Project channels rather than the official decision-making structures.

This should not be read as a cynical analysis. The employers and the unions wanted change. At various times during the Project it became evident that their visions had much in common, but neither wanted change that was conditional on the transfer of power to schools because of their fear that the other would re-acquire it. The Project teachers wanted change also, but not at any price. It was better to play the politician and produce an artful compromise than come up empty handed. The implicit deal (that is, the meta-rule) was that all the participants, department officials, union leaders and teachers in participating schools should get something out of it. This accommodation guaranteed the status quo.

Could the National Schools Project have worked? My conclusion is that it could only have worked had there been a re-alignment of powers between the central employer and union authorities on the one hand and schools on the other. The token relaxation of rules might have enabled some radical re-configurations of work organization but only temporarily. Eventually such schools would be re-subjected to the rule.

Can Schools Be Reformed by Regulation?

What are the prospects of carefully planned, fully resourced top–down reform? Some officials and scholars are optimistic under circumstances where the state has had the power to completely overhaul the regulatory framework. Proponents of the restructuring of the Kentucky public education system give it as an example of reform that was initiated from the top and that is working (see Steffy, 1993). Antagonists of the Education Reform Act in England and Wales take a contrary position. In each case regulatory revisions were far reaching. In reform programs of this kind, by producing a completely new set of rule regimes the reformers may avoid the problem of blending new and inconsistent, archaic residual rules. The new legal text is likely to be clearer about what has to change. The symbolism of state legitimation may be unambiguous (though not necessarily more helpful). And, practically, if the legislation and regulations have been cleverly drafted, the prospect of promulgating contradictory directives is reduced. However there can be no certainty that comprehensiveness of the regulatory package is the answer. The new regimes must still be integrated with other rule regimes that operate outside the ambit of the new legislation, and the district and school rules that are already in place. Equally important are the massive numbers of informal rules. If the objectives of the reform program are to be achieved then new social rule systems which are sympathetic to the reform objectives must emerge from this confluence of rules. As I have shown elsewhere, this is a complex process.

Regulatory reformers therefore find themselves confronting a classic Catch-22 situation. They want the rules to reach into schools yet, the broader the legislative revisions, the greater the disturbance to patterns of work organization and the more improbable that reforms will proceed smoothly. When complexity of the rule systems in schools is taken into account the idea of dovetailing a new set of rules with the old, carefully engineered with the new workplace in mind so that there is virtually no disturbance to the workplace, seems an unlikely prospect, a hyper-rationalist fantasy. Teachers may voluntarily or involuntarily change their practice, but disturbance of some kind or other follows. Inevitably there is a meshing of rules.

Rather than attempting to change the whole regulatory system, another strategy might be to target the official rules that frame teaching and then enforce them selectively. This approach was considered in Chapter 3. It is unclear whether the strategy works since most of the regulations relating to work organization have been put in place in order to solve administrative and collective bargaining problems rather than to address problems of teaching and learning. Hence, whether or not the strategy would work is partly an empirical question. Manipulating these rules can produce unintended negative consequences. It is like experimenting with the rigging on a sailing boat without knowing how the pulleys and winches work or the direction of the prevailing winds.

In drawing attention to this problem I am not arguing that all regulatory reform is ineffectual. For example, changing regulations governing who can become a teacher may have a net result of more suitable and competent teachers. However, if the basic structures that govern teachers' work organization and pedagogy are unchanged then the orthodox patterns of teaching are likely to endure since they are unrelated to changes in teacher competence. Forms of pedagogy which are contingent upon the adoption of different patterns of work organization and which utilize the competence in new ways will be found too hard to put into effect in the face of the institutionalized patterns of doing things. The regularities of schooling will persist.

What are the prospects of the reforms of choice, for example, fully deregulating schools by shifting power from central authorities to schools? This strategy is frequently debated, often in the context of demand-driven systems of resource allocation, but almost never happens. Schools in more limited regulatory reform programs designed to waive or abolish rules usually end up acquiring limited conditional powers but the broad powers of governance continue to be held centrally. Full deregulation would require the redefinition of the powers of the state in relation to school education. The dominant trend in political reform, however, has been for the centralization rather than decentralization of power. The reasons are political: the central authorities do not want to let go of the power to intervene in schools. Nor is there a political mandate to do so. There is the fear that school administrators, teachers or local governing bodies might abuse their powers and the state would be powerless to intervene.

The real dilemma for reformers who favour deregulation is the apparent contradiction between directing reform *and* devolving power locally. The differences between directing reform and controlling schools become confused during the tensions and uncertainties that arise when change is introduced. Practising the former and not the latter requires a level of deception. Practising the latter and not the former means that governments must surrender the control that they are expected to exercise without any certainty that such regulatory reform will make things better.

This analysis of regulatory reform has been more successful in explaining why things stay the same than how to make them different. Consider the options. Legislated changes have a low probability of meshing with the rule systems in use in schools in ways which would enable a healthy reorientation. Attempts to focus the official rules governing practice on agreed notions of good practice might produce the changes sought by the reformers or they might not. Exemptions from official rules which leave the power relations between the central agencies and the schools intact are likely to maintain the existing order in the system as a whole even if there are short-lived pockets of innovation. Finally, exemptions from official rules which legally empower schools to define their own forms of work organization and approaches to teaching, essentially by working outside the system, have some prospect of fundamentally reshaping work practice though it is doubtful whether there will ever be sufficient political appetite to make public schools fully self-regulating in such matters. This is a bleak conclusion for die-hard reformers. It suggests that the regularities of schooling are outside their control.

Regularities, Meta-rules and Values

If the interplay of meta-rules maintains the regularities found in education systems then a new question logically follows: What maintains the meta-rules? My speculative answer is that they are immanent in the very conception of a public education system. The meta-rules *are* the system, or at least indicative of its underlying structures. To undo the meta-rules would be to undo the system. This is not to say that it is impossible to imagine a public education system of self-determining schools with a variable pattern of work organization but that this would require a feat of imagination, not of administrative practice.

When we come to operationalize our thinking about the administration of public school systems we bring to the fore certain values and principles which are unquestioned organizers. Consider, for example, the value of equity. Most governments seek to provide a public education of comparable standard for the children of rich and poor alike. The significance of this value is evident in the historical accounts of the formation of public education systems.[2] The value of equity was administratively expressed through standardization. Officials, who see themselves as custodians of equality, use regulations to zealously guard its proxy, uniformity, to such an extent that equality, uniformity and regulation become fused together (see Cusick, 1992). It is easy to understand the persuasiveness of a doctrine which equates similitude of provision with fairness and a tendency to see any variations in provision as meaning that some children, either at the school where the variation is evident or elsewhere, must be getting more or less than some others.

A construction of equity which equates it with similitude of provision is at the core of the problem of regulatory reform. The rules that have been put in place to make public education systems equitable for teachers and students promote uniformity of teaching and learning conditions and contribute to the enduring patterns that reformers want to interrupt. The protective shell of work organization rules that protect teaching are such rules. But changes to these rules threaten the core values of public education. Some reformers want schools to preserve these rules *and* the values they reflect, yet make schools different. In my view, these are irreconcilable objectives.

I am not at this late stage of the book wanting to open up a Pandora's box of new issues. Nor is my purpose to take a position in the debate over choice of schooling or to attack the value of equity. What I am asserting is that core values that underpin public education, of which equity is only one, account, at least partially, for the regularities of schooling.[3] They are reflected in the social rule systems and the meta-rules that span them. If this is so, and the regularities are in effect reifications of these values, then it would be necessary to transform the constructions of those values found in the social and political systems which surround schools in order to break the mould of public education.

Notes

1 In an empirical study of attitudes towards the law Tyler (1990) concluded that people obey the law because they think it is proper to do so, that is they act not simply from self-interest.

2 In Australia, the shaping of present-day state education bureaucracies began in the latter half of the nineteenth century when the Australian colonies established education departments controlled by a minister and responsible to parliament. The departmental apparatus replaced the many semi-independent central and district boards responsible for administering colonial schools. Governments of the day believed that it was only by the exercise of central control and by the adoption of uniform standards that the newly formed states could provide adequate public education. Implicit in the thinking of central officials was the principle that students should be safeguarded from teacher errors of judgment or incompetence by requiring compliance of teachers and school officials with detailed sets of rules and standards. The resultant 'teacher-proofing' led to an increasing reliance among school staff on the rules and dependence on central authorities to solve problems that could not be resolved by compliance with the rules. The power of this system was greatly enhanced by coupling the system of rules to a vigorous inspectoral system — the original head of the new Western Australian Education Department was given the title 'Chief Inspector'. Hyams and Bessant (1972) claim that the culmination of this trend was an 'absolute bureaucratization' with a consequential 'deadening regimentation' which has endured. The school system, they claim, emphasized mechanical administrative efficiency rather than vitality and innovation. Experts from the US who visited Australia commented favourably on the uniformity of schools with

respect to their standards of staffing, curricular offerings and school buildings given the context of a sparsely-populated, arid continent. See for example, Butts (1964).

3   Garms *et al.* (1978) write that four of the values which compete for the attention of policy makers are equity, quality, efficiency and choice. I would add the value of 'order' to this list. All of these values are reflected in the administration of public school systems to some extent though the least prominent has been choice.

Appendix: Methodology

We live in a forest of symbols on the edge of a jungle of fact. (Gusfield, 1981)

Introduction

In this appendix, I describe the methodological viewpoint that I adopted during the study (or series of studies, to be more precise) and the empirical evidence that I employed to support my argument.

Theoretical Framework

There are plenty of references in the social sciences to rules. However, the 'facts' about rules do not add up. They only make sense in the theoretical context within which they have been framed. To take an extreme example, the phenomenological perspective that informs much of the sociological literature about informal rules and rule systems holds that there is no single, correct reading of the external world and no single way in which the 'facts' are to be selected and presented; such a position is the antithesis of the orthodox legal perspective in which 'the law' is set out in texts which have meanings defined through formal processes. My response has been to recognize the variation in perspectives rather than discard one or the other as 'false'.

Even within a single discipline area there are competing theories about rules and how people use them. I have taken the position that theories are worth using as long as they can explain some phenomenon. They do not have to explain all phenomena. For example, I believe that sometimes actions are rule-governed in a very literal and rational sense. People stop smoking in public places because of the sanctions for doing so. Thus, behaviourist theories provide an adequate means of explaining why people follow rules under certain conditions. But such theories do not explain adequately why people voluntarily allow others to act against their interests. On the other hand, theories of the state, which do so, are unnecessarily complex for the purpose of explaining compliance or non-compliance of teachers with rules governing smoking on school premises though no doubt it would be possible to regard these rules as part of the apparatus of state control.

The safest course would have been to adopt a particular theoretical framework from a key discipline area. I might have been able to represent most of what I wanted to write within the boundaries of social psychology and organizational theory; Burns and Flam (1987), whose work impressed me, for the most part kept within those boundaries. However, rule system theory did not go far enough for my purposes. Also, it is based on work that had run its course prior to the advent of post-structuralist thinking of the 1980s and later with an emphasis on language and 'discourse'. However, I resisted collapsing the whole study into an investigation of 'discourse', even though I recognize that this construct might have allowed me to represent rules as 'discursive practices' and to have written about school reform within a similar theoretical position to, say, that adopted by Thomas Popkewitz (1991) or Stephen Ball (1994). I wanted to retain a focus on rules even though I sense that contemporary academic work has moved on from the study of how actions are governed by rules, at least for the time being. I preferred the tangibility (perhaps the familiarity) of rules. The net result is a synthesis of theoretical positions. The notion of meta-rule has helped me bridge the constructs of rule systems and discourse without, I hope, either one being obfuscated by the other. Where has this left me? If I were pressed to locate the study within a single, overarching rubric, then I would describe the rubric as 'structuralist'.

Structuralist analyses are seductive because they simplify complex situations by revealing latent or hidden organizing principles or structures and suggest therefore that the analyst can see things that cannot ordinarily be seen by those immediately surrounded by the situation. In suggesting that school reform is shaped by a relatively small number of meta-rules this study has a decidedly structuralist bent. In exploring the construct of meta-rules I found some parallels with Chomsky's distinction between surface and deep structures and between the rules of linguistics.[1] This raises the question of whether meta-rules should be regarded as underlying structures which determine the responses of individuals and groups in particular situations. I am not going this far. I have not used the concept of meta-rules strictly in this sense. I am not hoping to uncover a universal set of rules which might be called the grammar of school reform (as Tyack and Tobin (1994), quoted in Chapter 4, have suggestively used the term). Nor am I suggesting that meta-rules form structures which preclude any independent action; the rules can be broken though there are consequences for doing so. My use of meta-rules is structuralist in some respects, however. The rules are shared and culturally embedded, and they are hierarchical or 'executive' in that the meta-rules subordinate other rules, but I do not see them forming a deep, unified structure in the sense of Chomsky or Levi-Strauss.

My reason for eschewing a deep structure of meta-rules arises from pragmatic grounds rather than from any theoretical opposition to structuralism; it is unnecessary. I am not trying to advance any universalistic claim of a reductionist kind — 'the arena of school reform is governed by 10 meta-rules, hitherto not revealed and here they are.'[2] I am suggesting that people do apply meta-rules as I have described them and that these are likely to shape the positions that teachers adopt in relation to school reform.

This begs the question of the number of meta-rules that *might* come into play. The answer is not straightforward. On balance, as I have indicated, I consider such a task of definitively listing them is not worth attempting.

First, some of the rules may be shared by some members though not by all. Meta-rules are social constructions. Because there are multiple discourses, and therefore multiple sets of meta-rules, a single list of meta-rules that operate in most workplaces would be artificial and potentially misleading. Large school systems are segmented and multicultural. For example, the 'atmospherics' of the central office are quite different from a school. So is the work. Just as there are multiple discourses in school systems so there will be multiple rule systems and sets of meta-rules. Teachers and central officials may know some of the meta-rules in the other's locality but that does not mean that they are guided by them. To sum up this point, I contend that studying meta-rules in order to understand the dynamics of the workplace can be helpful whereas producing a list and claiming it to be finite seems to me to be an unachievable enterprise.

Second, the rules may come into play only under certain conditions. People may not recognize the rule until it has been applied in some way and even then not be able to explain why they act the way they do. Psychologists, such as Piaget, have noted that people commonly can only give their reasons for doing something after the event.

There is a third problem of a different order: the number of rules that could be identified is contingent upon the level of analysis undertaken. The observer can stand close to the action, as it were, and find a potentially large number of 'executive' rules about what constitutes an appropriate action or utterance in the same way that sociolinguists can analyse a minute's interaction between members of a group and convert it into a Proustian commentary of what is actually taking place. Alternatively, the dynamics of a workplace may be described in terms of a small set of organizing principles *àpropos* F. Neil Brady's suggestion that managers are ultimately guided by *two* meta-rules. As Wittgenstein has pointed out there are rules about rules about rules leading to an infinite regress. However, many meta-rules are identified and whatever their scope or generality there are, presumably, rules about how such meta-rules are brought into play.

My response is basically utilitarian: the meta-rules should be defined at what ever level and scope is helpful to understanding some event or process. I am eschewing the classical structuralist hope that by dint of thoughtful and persistent investigation ultimately, beneath the surface layer of rules will be revealed a deeper structure of rules — meta-rules — which apply universally across cultures and situations.

The Empirical Evidence Supporting the Argument

Interviews with Departmental and Union Officials

In 1993, I was funded by Edith Cowan University (Grant No. A-302–074) to undertake a study which would 'map the key features of the regulatory framework which defines acceptable forms of work organization in Australian school systems'. This aim was to be accomplished by analysing relevant statutes, awards and ordinances collected from education authorities. In addition, key union and employer officials who held responsibility for regulatory reform were to be interviewed with regard to the perceptions of the adequacy of the regulatory framework. My entry point was to be through the members of the Governing Board of the National Project on the Quality of Teaching and Learning which had oversight of the National Schools Project. All states and territories agreed to participate. I conducted the interviews during March to December 1993 and during my visits to the headquarters of these bodies collected the relevant documentation.

I had planned to interview only a single union and a departmental official from each of the eight states and territories in Australia, however, I conducted a further eight interviews with legal and industrial specialists in order to elaborate technical matters or matters of detail. With regard to the sixteen 'official' interviews, I sought to meet with the most senior official available, preferably directors general or union presidents. In fact, of the sixteen interviews, two were with directors general and seven with state union presidents. The others held senior positions in their organizations. Seven of the sixteen were members of the Governing Board of the NPQTL.

The interviews were approximately of an hour's duration and tape-recorded. All were conducted on a face-to-face basis except for telephone interviews with the Northern Territory interviewees. The interviews were broadly structured around a series of issues: the adequacy of the Westminster system, the state of the current regulatory system, the specification of work organization regulations, devolution and the use of delegated powers, exemption from regulation, the nexus between educational and industrial matters, and the extent to which official rules were perceived to constrain practice.

I have used the information collected from this study to compile the description of official rules contained in Chapter 2. Elsewhere in the book, when I refer to the attitudes and beliefs of senior officials about regulation, and quote them directly, I am drawing on the interview transcripts.

At a more general level, I have supplemented this interview data with notes and reflections arising from my own experience as a senior official in the Education Department of Western Australia. I have also used the interviews to supplement my account of the National Schools Project although much of what I have written on this topic is drawn from my first-hand experience as a member of the Governing Board of the National Project on the Quality of Teaching and Learning and, more particularly, as chair of the national steering committee for the National Schools Project. As well, I referred to comprehensive records of this period which I had retained.

Survey of National Schools Project Pilot Schools

In May 1994, using a register supplied by the National Schools Network, I surveyed the 169 pilot schools that had participated during 1993 in the

National Schools Project. A total of 116 responses (68.6 per cent) were received by the cut-off date in early July.

The survey instrument contained four blocks of questions and a space within each block for written comment. The first block of questions was designed to find out whether schools had discarded or deferred proposals to improve teaching and learning 'even though they seemed to have merit and had broad staff support'. If they answered in the affirmative, respondents were asked to give examples. The second block inquired whether there were 'any policies, regulations, or industrial agreements which prevented [the respondent] from developing or implementing a project to improve teaching and learning?' If the answer was affirmative, respondents were asked whether they tried to exempt their school from the policy, regulation or agreement, and if so, whether they gained an exemption. In the third block respondents were asked whether their proposals were approved by the state steering committee and if not, why not. Finally, respondents were asked to comment generally about the impediments that they encountered when implementing their plans and ideas.

The results of the survey were coded and cross-tabulated. The written comments, containing examples of project proposals that gained exemption or were denied exemption, were transcribed and catalogued along with general comments about the Project. I have used the results of the survey to support my conclusions about the efficacy of regulatory reform involving exemptions.

Case Studies of School Staff Knowledge and Use of Rules

I draw on several occasions on the Master of Education thesis of Ray Knight, *The Interplay of Formal and Informal Rule Systems in Government Primary Schools.* Knight conducted case studies of two suburban primary schools and framed his study according to the rule system theory of Burns and Flam (1987). The data were collected throughout the 1994 school year. Knight sought to find out how much teachers and school administrators know about the official rules and how informal rules supplement a partial knowledge of the official rules.

To address these questions, Knight surveyed the twenty-nine staff in the two schools about rules, formally tested the knowledge about the official rules of these twenty-nine staff members and then followed up with consecutive, focused interviews with twelve of the same staff. Finally, he interviewed the district superintendent about the same matters.

I have used Knight's study principally to supplement the evidence that I collected from senior officials about knowledge of the official rules. Though based only on two schools, the responses of teachers support my claims that the official rules are not well known and yet the schools function as though they are rule governed. Of course, generalizing from two schools is hazardous. I can imagine that there are some schools where staff, for a variety of reasons, are highly rule conscious. Nevertheless, the results of Knight's study are consistent with the comments of the officials and also my own experience as a departmental official.

Illustrating Meta-rules

At the beginning of 1996, I received a grant from Edith Cowan University (A-320–140) to examine how meta-rules shape work practices. This study is still in progress, however, I have been able to use interview transcripts from it to illustrate informal rules and the emergence of meta-rules.

During 1996, fifteen teachers, school administrators and union and departmental officials were interviewed about their recent involvement in school reform. The purpose of the interviews was to explicate meta-rules that had overridden the formal and informal rules that generally applied. The interviews were open ended. In some cases I introduced the idea of meta-rules and sought examples although generally I probed for 'underlying principles' that explained why events had unfolded in a particular way. Evidence from this study has been cited or quoted in Chapters 7, 8 and 9.

Autobiographical Evidence

I have occasionally interpolated into the study illustrations drawn from my own experience. Until recently, I would have been reluctant to do this. The use of the first person and anecdotal evidence, I used to think, breached inviolable canons of method. Such practices implied subjectivity. I feel differently about this issue now. On a purely practical level it seems wasteful to ignore insights derived from personal experience and dishonest not to disclose their origin. I doubt whether it makes much difference whether an account is drawn from observations and reflection from the immediate, documented past (called research) or from the more distant, less scrupulously documented past (called reminiscence or autobiography). Both are interpretive acts and are liable to the distortions of self interest, forgetfulness and blinkered perceptiveness, that is, plain bias. One of the reasons for the truncated autobiographical beginning to the book was to declare my own position and its origins.

Representing the Evidence

Something else that I have done in this study, but in earlier years would have been reluctant to do, is combine different data sources, particularly interviews, conducted during the period 1993 to 1996. The earlier interviews with senior officials took place before I had fully formulated my ideas on meta-rules. I am assuming that attitudes and beliefs about rules in general are relatively stable. I am not attempting to map how a particular rule has become more or less salient as well it might. Similarly, a particular meta-rule may have decayed or been abruptly changed as a consequence of a substantial re-alignment of power, however, other meta-rules would still come into play and shape the response to school reform proposals as I have described.

Readability has been a primary objective in writing this book. I have also sought to avoid cluttering it with lengthy, verbatim excerpts from interview transcripts which can easily become tedious and distracting. So can obsessive referencing. I have not affixed codes to each utterance that I have quoted. Readers should therefore adopt the general principle that direct quotations of senior officials have been drawn from my 1993 interviewing program and that quotations of teachers and school administrators have been drawn from my 1996 study of meta-rules. When I quote from Ray Knight's 1994 study I indicate that I have done so.

Illustration versus Verification

I have used the empirical evidence in this study to illustrate the various propositions in my argument. I do not pretend that the 'data', mainly excerpts from interviews, allow me to present an empirical 'proof' that meta-rules function the way I have described though they add a measure of plausibility. Presumably, were I persistent enough I could have ambled around with a tape-recorder and eventually found someone who would say what suited my purpose. I chose not to draw structured samples or report the percentages of responses to pre-considered questions. My argument does not hinge upon demonstrating that all teachers, or a certain proportion of teachers or officials from the population of teachers and officials, share a common point of view. The validity of my argument, remembering that it is an argument not only about rules but also about rules *and* school reform, does depend upon the coherence of its parts as well as the empirical evidence that I have assembled.

This raises questions relating to the validity of constructs such as rule systems, meta-rules and discourse. I have defined them into existence and they are hard to illustrate adequately. Basically, my 'data' is text and speech but each of the core concepts is more than a piece of each or a mixture of both. The problem is compounded by the tacit quality of rules and discourse. Do meta-rules exist? My answer is 'yes' if there is inter-subjective agreement among members of an organization. I found that when talking with teachers or officials, and to provide a context for the discussion, that if I suggested a meta-rule in the form of a proposition, operating principle, or anecdote about 'how the system really worked', my informants were quick to pick up on the idea and accept, refine or reject it. The rule may have been tacit because it was unconscious, that is, was never reflected upon, or because it was considered politically naive, or even politically incorrect, to refer to it in public.

I recognize the questions about whether my arguments can be generalized. Most of the data that I have used is drawn from the Western Australian public school system. I have no doubt that within that system attitudes towards authority vary and that in some schools the official rules are used quite differently. However, I am not arguing that particular meta-rules apply universally across the various parts of the system or that they are always observed. I am arguing that in every system informal and official rules combine to constitute social rule systems and that there are meta-rules which provide the overarching expectancies of how teachers and officials should respond to reform.

Notes

1   For a general overview of structuralism, see Sturrock (1993). What might be described as 'pure' structuralism, of the kind associated with perhaps its foremost practitioner, Claude Levi-Strauss, has had its heyday. The field is no longer engaged by attempts to show that the basic structures of the human mind can be revealed by uncovering the phonemic structures of myths. For a sharp-edged criticism of structuralism, read Eagleton, 1983. Yet, as Sturrock points out, insofar as *post*-structuralism represents the new academic wisdom, it builds upon rather than repudiates many of the core ideas that have underpinned structuralist thinking. For example, the post-structuralist notion of 'discourse', which I employ, has its roots it structuralist theories of language.
2   I have in mind the kind of structuralism made famous by Propp (1968), who reduced all folktales to seven spheres of action and thirty-one fixed elements or functions.

References

AHS, K. (1986) 'UTRES — Evaluation of resource utilisation in upper secondary school', *School Research Newsletter No 3*, Stockholm, Swedish National Board of Education.

ANGUS, M.J. (1992) *Chinese Whispers: The Transformation of Knowledge about Teaching*, Geelong: Deakin University Press.

ANGUS, M.J., BECK, T., HILL, P. and MCATEE, W. (1979) *A National Study of Open Area Schools*, Canberra: Australian Government Print Service.

AUSTRALIAN EDUCATION COUNCIL (1989) *Common and Agreed Goals for Schooling in Australia*, Melbourne: Australian Education Council.

BACHRACH, P. and BARATZ, M.S. (1970) *Power and Poverty: Theory and Practice*, New York: Oxford University Press.

BALL, S. (1994) *Education Reform: A Critical and Post-structural Approach*, Buckingham: Open University Press.

BAUMAN, Z. (1990) *Thinking Sociologically*, Oxford: Blackwell.

BERNIER, I. and LAJOIE, A. (eds) (1985) *Regulations, Crown Corporations and Administrative Tribunals*, Toronto: University of Toronto.

BIRCH, I. (1993) *Law and Educational Planning*, Paris: UNESCO, International Institute for Educational Planning.

BIRCH, I. (1976) *The School and the Law*, Melbourne: University Press.

BIRCH, I. and RICHTER, I. (1990) *Comparative School Law*, Oxford: Pergamon.

BITTNER, E. (1967) 'The police on skid-row: A study of peace keeping', *American Sociological Review*, **32**, pp. 699–715.

BOON, J. (1986) 'Symbols, sylphs and siwa: Allegorical machineries in the text of Balinese culture', in TURNER, V.M. and BRUNER, E.M. (eds) *The Anthropology of Experience*, Urbana: University of Illinios Press.

BOSCH, H. (1990) *The Workings of a Watchdog*, Melbourne: William Heinemann Australia.

BRADY, F. (1987) 'Rules for making exceptions to rules', *Academy of Management Review*, **12**, 3, pp. 436–44.

BURNS, T. and FLAM, H. (1987) *The Shaping of Social Organisation: Social Rule System Theory with Applications*, London: Sage.

BUTTS, R.F. (1964) *Assumptions Underlying Australian Education*, Melbourne: Australian Council for Educational Research.

CENTRAL MICHIGAN UNIVERSITY (1996) *Understanding Charter Schools: The CMU Charter Schools Initiative*, Mount Pleasant: Michigan, Author.

CHISOLM, R. (ed.) (1987) *Teachers, Schools and the Law in New South Wales*, Kensington, Sydney: New South Wales University Press.

CHITTY, C. and SIMON, B. (eds) (1993) *Education Answers Back: Critical Responses to Government Policy*, London: Lawrence and Wishart.

CHRISTIE, G. (1982) *Law, Norms and Society*, London: Duckworth.

CHUBB, J. and MOE, T. (1990) *Politics, Markets and America's Schools*, Washington, DC: The Brooking Institute.

COHEN, D. (1988) 'Teaching practice, plus ça change . . .', in JACKSON, P. (ed.) *Contributing to Educational Change*, Berkeley, CA: McCutchen Publishing Corporation.

COHEN, D. and GRANT, S. (1993) 'America's children and their elementary schools', *Daedalus*, **122**, 1, pp. 177–207.

COHEN, D. and SPILLANE, J. (1992) 'Policy and practice: The relations between governance and instruction', in GRANT, G. (ed.) *Review of Research in Education*, **18**, Washington, DC: American Educational Research Association, pp. 3–49.

CONSIDINE, M. (1988) 'The Corporate Management Framework as Administrative Science', *Australian Journal of Public Administration*, **47**, pp. 4–18.

CUBAN, L. (1984) *How Teachers Taught: Constancy and Change in American Classrooms 1895–1989*, New York: Longman.

CUBAN, L. (1990) 'Reforming again, again and again', *Educational Researcher*, **19**, 1, pp. 3–13.

CUSICK, P. (1992) *The Educational System: Its Nature and Logic*, New York: McGraw Hill.

DAHLLOF, U. (1971) *Ability Grouping, Content Validity and Curriculum Process Analysis*, New York: Teachers College Press.

DAUDI, P. (1986) *Power in the Organisation: The Discourse of Power in Managerial Praxis*, London: Basil Blackwell.

DAVIS, J. (1989) 'Effective schools, organisational culture, and local policy initiatives', in HOLMES, M., LEITHWOOD, K.A. and MUSELLA, D.F. (eds) *Educational Policy for Effective Schools*, Toronto: OISE Press.

DEPARTMENT OF OCCUPATIONAL HEALTH, SAFETY AND WELFARE (1988) *Occupational Health, Safety and Welfare: Legislative Guidelines*, Perth: Department of Occupational.

DUDLEY, J. and VIDOVICH, L. (1995) *The Politics of Education: Commonwealth Schools Policy 1973–1995*, Melbourne: Australian Council of Educational Research.

EAGLETON, T. (1995) 'The death of self-criticism', *Times Literary Supplement*, November 24, p. 7.

EAGLETON, T. (1983) *Literary Theory: An Introduction*, Oxford: Blackwell.

EDUCATION DEPARTMENT OF SOUTH AUSTRALIA (1988) *Administrative Instructions and Guidelines*, Adelaide: Education Department of South Australia.

EDUCATION DEPARTMENT OF WESTERN AUSTRALIA (1960) *Education Act Regulations*, Perth: Government Printer.

EDUCATION DEPARTMENT OF WESTERN AUSTRALIA (1994) *Student Outcome Statements*, East Perth: Education Department of Western Australia.

ELMORE, R.F. (1995) 'Teaching, learning and school organisation: Principles of practice and the regularities of schooling', *Educational Administration Quarterly*, **31**, 3, pp. 355–74.

ELMORE, R.F. and FUHRMAN, S.H. (eds) (1994) *The Governance of Curriculum, 1994 Yearbook of the Association for Supervision and Curriculum Development*, Alexandria, Virginia: ASCD.

FEINTUCK, M. (1994) *Accountability and Choice In Schooling*, Buckingham: Open University Press.

FOUCAULT, M. (1979) *The History of Sexuality: An Introduction*, Harmondsworth: Penguin.

FOUCAULT, M. (1984) 'How is power exercised?', in WALLIS, B. and TUCKER, M. (eds) *Art after Modernism: Rethinking Representation*, New York: Museum of Contemporary Art.

FRY, P., FUHRMAN, S.H. and ELMORE, R.F. (1992) *Schools for the 21st Century Program in Washington State: A Case Study*, New Brunswick, NJ: Consortium for Policy Research in Education.

FUHRMAN, S.H. (1994) 'Legislatures and education policy', in ELMORE, R.F. and FUHRMAN, S.H. (eds) *The Governance of Curriculum, 1994 Yearbook of the Association for Supervision and Curriculum Development*, Alexandria, Virginia: ASCD.

FUHRMAN, S.H. (ed.) (1993) *Designing Coherent Policy: Improving the System*, San Francisco: Jossey-Bass.

FUHRMAN, S.H., CLUNE, W.H. and ELMORE, R.F. (1988) 'Research on educational reform: Lessons on the implementation of policy', *Teachers College Record*, **90**, pp. 237–57.

FUHRMAN, S.H., FRY, P. and ELMORE, R. (1992) *South Carolina's Flexibility Through Deregulation Program: A Case Study*, New Brunswick, NJ, Rutgers University: Consortium for Policy Research in Education.

FULLAN, M. (1992) *The New Meaning of Educational Change*, New York: Teachers College Press.

GALLIGAN, D.J. (1990) *Discretionary Powers: A Legal Study of Official Discretion*, Oxford: Clarendon.

GARMS, W., GUTHRIE, J. and PIERCE, L. (1978) *School Finance: The Economics and Politics of Education*, Englewood Cliffs, NJ: Prentice Hall.

GEERTZ, C. (1973) *The Interpretation of Cultures*, New York: Basic Books.

GEERTZ, C. (1983) *Local Knowledge: Further Essays in Interpretive Anthropology*, New York: Basic Books.

GERSTNER, L., SEMERAD, D., DOYLE, D. and JOHNSTON, W. (1994) *Reinventing Education: Entrepreneurship in America's Public Schools*, New York: Dutton.

GILBERT, R. (1991) *Reglomania: The Curse of Organisational Reform and How to Cure It*, Sydney: Prentice Hall.

GITLIN, A. and MARGONIS, F. (1995) 'The political aspect of reform: Teacher resistance as good sense,' *American Journal of Education*, **103**, pp. 377–405.

GOODLAD, J. (1984) *A Place Called School: Prospects for the Future*, New York: McGraw Hill.

GORE, A. (1993) *From Red Tape to Results: Creating a Government that Works Better and Costs Less*, New York: Times Books.

GUSFIELD, J. (1981) *The Culture of Public Problems: Drink-Driving and the Symbolic Order*, Chicago: University of Chicago Press.

HANUSHEK, E. (1994) 'Money might matter somewhere: A response to Hedges, Laine and Greenwald', *Educational Researcher*, **23**, 4, pp. 5–8.

HARGREAVES, A. (1994) *Changing Teachers, Changing Times: Teachers' Work and Culture in the Postmodern Age*, London: Cassell.

HARGREAVES, D. (1994) 'The new professionalism: The synthesis of professional and institutional development', *Teaching and Teacher Education*, **10**, pp. 423–38.

HARRADINE, J. (1996) 'What research tells us about school reform', *National Schools Network Newsletter*, **2**, pp. 4–5.

HEDGES, L., LAINE, R. and GREENWALD, R. (1994) 'Does money matter? A meta-analysis of studies of the effects of differential school inputs on student outcomes', *Educational Researcher*, **23**, 3, pp. 5–14.

HOY, D. (1992) 'Power, repression, progress: Foucault, Lukes and the Frankfurt School', in HOY, D. (ed.) *Foucault: A Critical Reader*, Oxford: Blackwell.

HYAMS, B. and BESSANT, B. (1972) *Schools for the People: An Introduction to the History of State Education in Australia*, Hawthorn, Victoria: Longman.

JACKSON, P. (1968) *Life in Classrooms*, New York: Holt, Rinehart and Winston.

JENKINS, E. (1995) 'Central policy and teacher response? Scientific investigation in the national curriculum of England and Wales', *International Journal of Science Education*, **17**, 4, pp. 471–79.

JONES, A. (1970) *Memorandum to Heads of Departmental Schools: Freedom and Authority in Schools*, Education Department of South Australia.

KEESING, R. (1987) 'Anthropology as interpretive text', *Current Anthropology*, **28**, pp. 161–62.

KIRST, M.W. and MEISTER, G.R. (1985) 'Turbulence in American high schools: What reforms last?', *Curriculum Inquiry*, **15**, pp. 169–86.

KNIGHT, R. (1996) *The Interplay of Formal and Informal Rule Systems in Government Primary Schools*, Master of Education Thesis, Edith Cowan University, Perth.

KNOTT, A., TRONC, K. and MIDDLETON, J. (1980) *Australian Schools and the Law: Principal, Teacher and Student*, Brisbane: University of Queensland Press.

LADWIG, J., CURRIE, J. and CHADBOURNE, R. (1994) *Toward Rethinking Australian Schools: A Synthesis of the Reported Practices of the National Schools Project*, Sydney: National Schools Network.

LAING, R.D. (1976) *The Politics of the Family and other Essays*, Harmondsworth: Penguin.

LEVACIC, R. (1995) *Local Management of Schools: Analysis and Practice*, Buckingham: Open University Press.

LINDBLOM, C.E. (1990) *Inquiry and Change: The Troubled Attempt to Understand and Shape Society*, New Haven, CT: Yale University Press.

LOUIS, K. and MILES, M. (1990) *Improving the Urban High School: What Works and Why*, New York: Teachers College Press.

LUKES, S. (1974) *Power: A Radical View*, London: Macmillan.

LUNDGREN, U. (1972) *Frame Factors and the Teaching Process*, Stockholm: Almquist and Wicksell.

LUNDGREN, U. (1979) 'Educational evaluation: A basis for, or legitimation of, educational policy', *Scandinavian Journal of Educational Research*, **23**, pp. 31–45.

LUNDGREN, U. (1983) 'Social production and reproduction as a context for curriculum theorizing', *Journal of Curriculum Studies*, **15**, 2, pp. 143–54.

LUNDGREN, U. (1986) 'Education — society: Curricular theory', *School Research Newsletter No. 1*, Stockholm, Swedish National Board of Education.

MACDONALD, R. (1985) 'Understanding regulation by regulation', in BERNIER, I. and LAJOIE, A. (eds) *Regulations, Crown Corporations and Administrative Tribunals*, Toronto: University of Toronto Press.

MACHIAVELLI, N. (1975) 'In what ways princes must keep faith', in BARRICELLI, J-P. *Machiavelli's 'The Prince': Text and Commentary*, New York: Barron's Educational Series.

MALEN, B., OGAWA, R. and KRANZ, J. (1990) What do we know about school-based management: A case study of the literature', in CLUNE, W.H. and WITTE, J.F. (eds) *Choice and Control in American Education Volume 2*, London: Falmer Press.

MARSHALL, C., MITCHELL, D. and WIRT, E. (1989) *Culture and Education Policy in the American States*, London: Falmer Press.

MAZIBUKO, E. (1996) *The Mediation of Teaching Through Central Curriculum Controls: Four Case Studies of History Teaching in Year 12 in Western Australia*, Ph.D. dissertation, Edith Cowan University, Perth.

MCLAUGHLIN, M. (1990) 'The Rand Change Agent Study revisited: Macro perspective and micro realities', *Educational Researcher*, **19**, 9, pp. 11–17.

MCNEIL, L.M. (1988) *Contradictions of Control: School Structures and School Knowledge*, New York: Routledge.

MEHAN, H. and WOOD, H. (1975) *The Reality of Ethnomethodology*, New York: John Wiley and Sons.

MEIER, D. (1995) *The Power of Their Ideas*, Boston: Beacon Press.

MEYER, J.W. (1986) 'Organizational factors affecting legalization in education', in KIRP, D.L. and JENSEN, D.N. (eds) *School Days, Rule Days: The Legalization and Regulation of Education*, London: Falmer Press.

MILLS, A. and MURGATROYD, S. (1991) *Organizational Rules: A Framework for Understanding Organizational Action*, Buckingham: Open University Press.

MINISTRY OF EDUCATION, WESTERN AUSTRALIA (n.d.) 'The managing change in schools project: A summary report on 1988 activities for involved unions', Unpublished document. The report was compiled by a teacher nominated by the union to liaise with the seven schools.

MINISTRY OF EDUCATION, WESTERN AUSTRALIA (1990) *Principals in Pursuit of Excellence*, Perth: Ministry of Education, Western Australia.

MIREL, J. (1994) 'School reform unplugged: The Bensenville New American Schools Project 1991–1993', *American Educational Research Journal*, **31**, 3, pp. 481–581.

NATIONAL SCHOOLS NETWORK (1995) *Schools Register: Project Descriptions*, Ryde, NSW: New South Wales Department of School Education.

NEW SOUTH WALES DEPARTMENT OF SCHOOL EDUCATION (1993) *Teacher's Handbook*, Sydney: New South Wales Department of School Education.

ODDEN, A., and MARSH, D. (1988) 'How comprehensive reform legislation can improve secondary schools', *Phi Delta Kappan*, **69**, 8, pp. 593–98.

OFFICE OF SCHOOLS ADMINISTRATION, VICTORIA (1990) *Schools Information Manual: School Operations*, Melbourne: Ministry of Education.

OGAWA, R.T., and WHITE, P.A. (1994) 'School-based management: An overview', in MOHRMAN, S.A. and WOHLSTETTER, P. *School-based Management: Organising for High Performance*, San Francisco: Jossey-Bass.

OSBORNE, D. and GAEBLER, T. (1992) *Reinventing Government: How the Entrepreneurial Spirit is Transforming the Public Sector*, New York: Addison Wesley.

PAUL (1952) 'Letter to the Hebrews', in *The Holy Bible Containing the Old and New Testaments: Revised Standard Version*, London: Wm Collins & Sons.

PETERSON, P.L., MCCARTHEY, S.J. and ELMORE, R.F. (1996) 'Learning from school restructuring', *American Educational Research Journal*, **33**, 1, pp. 119–53.

POPKEWITZ, T.S. (1991) *A Political Sociology of Educational Reform: Power/Knowledge in Teaching, Teacher Education, and Research*, New York: Teachers College Press.

POWELL, A., FARRAR, E. and COHEN, D. (1985) *The Shopping Mall High School*, Boston: Houghton Mifflin.

PROPP, V. (1968) *The Morphology of the Folktale*, Austin: Texas University Press.

RAND CORPORATION (1978) *Federal Programs Supporting Change and Sustaining Innovation*, Santa Monica, CA: Rand Corporation.

REARDON, D. (1996) 'Cap numbers: Teachers', *The West Australian*, 9 December, Perth, West Australian Newspapers.

ROSEBERRY, W. (1989) *Anthropologists and Histories: Essays in Culture, History and Political Economy*, New Brunswick: Rutgers University Press.

ROSENHOLTZ, S. (1988) *Teachers' Workplace*, New York: Longman.

SARASON, S. (1982) *The Culture of the School and the Problem of Change*, Boston: Allyn & Bacon.

SCHWILLE, J., PORTER, A., BELLI, G., FLODEN, R., FREEMAN, D., KNAPPEN, L., KUHS, T. and SCHMIDT, W. (1983) 'Teachers as policy brokers in the content of elementary school mathematics', in SHULMAN, L.S. and SYKES, G. (eds) *Handbook of Teaching and Policy*, New York: Longman.

SEDDON, T. (ed.) (1996) *Pay, Professionalism and Politics*, Melbourne: Australian Council for Educational Research.

SHERIF, M. (1965) *The Psychology of Social Norms*, New York: Octagon Books.

SHORTEN, A. (1995) 'The statutory framework of education and legal issues of concern for school administrators', in EVERS, C. and CHAPMAN, J. (eds) *Educational Administration: An Australian Perspective*, Sydney: Allen and Unwin.

SHULMAN, L.S. (1983) 'Autonomy and obligation: The remote control of teaching', in SHULMAN, L.S. and SYKES, G. (eds) *Handbook of Teaching and Policy*, New York: Longman.

SIROTNIK, K.A. (1983) 'What you see is what you get — consistency, persistency, and mediocrity in the classrooms', *Harvard Educational Review*, **53**, pp. 16–31.

STEFFY, B. (1993) *The Kentucky Education Reform: Lessons for America*, Lancaster, PA: Technomic Publishing.

STURROCK, J. (1993) *Structuralism*, London: Fontana.

SWIFT, J. (1969) *Gulliver's Travels*, Chicago: Children's Press.

THOMPSON, J.B. (1990) *Ideology and Modern Cutlure*, London: Polity Press.

TYACK, D. and CUBAN, L. (1995) *Tinkering Toward Utopia: A Century of Public School Reform*, Cambridge, MA: Harvard University Press.

TYACK, D. and TOBIN, W. (1994) 'The "grammar" of schooling: Why has it been so hard to change?', *American Educational Research Journal*, **31**, 3, pp. 453–79.

TYLER, T. (1990) *Why People Obey the Law*, New Haven, CT: Yale University Press.

WALKER, P.A. and RODER, L. (1993) 'Reflections on the practical and legal implications of school-based management and teacher empowerment', *Journal of Law and Education*, **22**, 2, pp, 159–75.

WEATHERLEY, R. and LIPSKY, M. (1977) 'Street-level bureaucrats and institutional innovation: Implementing special-education reform', *Harvard Educational Review*, **47**, pp. 171–99.

WEBER, M. (1978) 'The concept of following a rule', in RUNCIMAN, W.G. (ed.) and MATHEWS, E. (Trans.) *Max Weber: Selections in Translation*, Cambridge: Cambridge University Press.

WIEDER, D.L. (1970) 'On meaning by rule', in DOUGLAS, J.D. (ed.) *Understanding Everyday Life: Toward the Reconstruction of Sociological Knowledge*, Chicago: Aldine Publishing Company.

WILDAVSKY, A. (1979) *Speaking Truth to Power: The Art and Craft of Policy Analysis*, Boston: Little, Brown and Company.

WILLETTON SENIOR HIGH SCHOOL (1988) *Managing Change in Schools Project: Report of Outcomes to December 1988*, Willetton: Willetton Senior High School.

WILSON, J. (1988) *Bureaucracy: What Government Agencies Do and Why They Do It*, New York: Basic Books.

WISE, A. (1990) 'Student welfare in the era of school reform: Legislated learning revisited', in BACHARACH, S. (ed.) *Education Reform*, Boston: Allyn & Bacon.

WOHLSTETTER, P. (1994) 'Education by charter', in MOHRMAN, S.A. and WOHLSTETTER, P. (eds) *School-based Management: Organizing for High Performance*, San Francisco: Jossey-Bass.

WOHLSTETTER, P., WENNING, R. and BRIGGS, K.L. (1995) 'Charter schools in the United States: The question of autonomy', *Educational Policy*, **9**, 4, pp. 331–58.

WOOD, D. and BECK, R.J. (1994) *Home Rules*, Baltimore: John Hopkins University Press.

YANOW, D. (1987) 'Toward a policy culture approach to implementation', *Policy Studies Review*, **7**, 1, pp. 103–15.

Index